KIT CARSON'S LONG WALK

AND OTHER TRUE TALES
OF OLD SAN DIEGO

Henry Schwartz

Illustrated by AMY SCHWARTZ

ASSOCIATED CREATIVE WRITERS
9231 Molly Woods Ave.,
La Mesa, CA 92041

Kit Carson's Long Walk and Other True Tales of Old San Diego, by Henry Schwartz

Copyright © 1980, by Associated Creative Writers

Published by Associated Creative Writers
9231 Molly Woods Ave.,
La Mesa, CA 92041

Manufactured in U.S.A.

Library of Congress Catalog Card No.: 80-68570

ISBN 0-933362-03-X 395

80 81 82 83 84 85 86 9 8 7 6 5 4 3 2 1

**KIT CARSON'S
LONG WALK**

"THE WOLF WILL ESCAPE"

IN THE SUMMER OF 1842, a man who stood no taller than a buffalo's eyes boarded the *Rowena* in St. Louis. On the deck of the paddle-wheeler, he met Captain John C. Fremont, who was embarking on his first western exploration to chart the wilds from Missouri to the Rocky Mountains.

Fremont told the stranger that he had all his supplies, equipment, and men for this government topographical venture— he had everything except a guide. Then he asked the stranger did he know of anyone to guide his expedition.

In a soft voice, the short stranger applied for the job himself. Taken back by this improbable applicant, the captain inquired if he had experience on the frontier.

Whereupon the man spat out into the Mississippi, fixed Captain Fremont with steady, blue eyes, and replied: "I reckon so. A ten-prong buck warn't done suckin' when I last sit on a chair."

The short stranger was Kit Carson. He told Fremont with his usual modesty that he had been some time in the mountains. Actually, the 32-year-old Carson had lived the previous thirteen years in the wilderness, where white men were virtually unknown— and without the comfort of chairs. He had run away to the west in 1826 as a tow-headed lad of sixteen, his head filled with wild tales of hunting and "Injuns," as he called them.

He got the job. Carson went on to become a premier guide, perhaps the greatest of them all. He

Kit Carson

crossed and recrossed the mountains and deserts until he could find his way without a compass. He could parlay with Apaches in their own tongue or fight them to a standstill. Cool and endlessly resourceful in a crisis, he had survived dozens of desperate battles. In a pinch, he could survive for days merely by chewing on his buckskin leggings.

Yet, Carson struck new acquaintances like Fremont as an unlikely woodsman. An unheroic figure, he stood no higher than five and a half feet, was bandy-legged, and never weighed over a hundred and forty pounds. Later, the myth-makers touched up his exploits; Carson himself allowed that one popular biographer had "laid it on a leetle too thick." Inevitably, he faced incredulous stares.

One hero-worshipper was flabbergasted. He fully expected to meet a six-foot-plus Hercules, with the beard of Moses and the voice of an aroused lion. "The real Kit Carson," he found "to be a plain, simple, unostentatious man, rather below medium height, with brown, curling hair, little or no beard, and a voice as soft and gentle as a woman's."

Kit Carson was a plain man. He never learned to read or write, except to scratch out his name. Best understood as a Mountain Man, he hunted, trapped, and guided tenderfeet for a living. He scorned soft living and grew restless in civilized surroundings. Like other Mountaineers, he fancied himself a "white Injun." And when he felt it high time to marry, he chose a beautiful Arapaho maiden.

Nor was he free from frontier bias. Before he knew better as a result of the battle of San Pasqual, he thought Mexicans fought like old women. He fought hostile Indians fiercely. In his violent time, he followed the harsh frontier creed that dead braves were the price of safety.

Yet he was no Indian exterminator. A few months before his death, he recoiled at the butchery of Colonel Chivington's militia at Sand Creek, Colorado. "To think of that dog Chivington and his hounds, up thar at Sand Creek!...I never yet drew bead on a squaw or papoose and hate the man that would. Tain't nateral...and no one but a coward or dog would ever do it."

When not fighting Indians, he was their friend.

Redmen trusted him as they did few palefaces. His
word was his bond. As an Indian agent and a negotia-
tor in concluding peace with the Great Plains Indians, he accomplished a lot. His well-known Indian
sympathies led the Senate to refuse to confirm his
field commission as a lieutenant in the U. S. Army.
In the Civil War, however, when the North desperate-
ly needed the likes of Kit Carson, they made him a
brigadier general.

II

KIT CARSON'S SAN DIEGO ADVENTURES began in trav-
esty and ended in a desperate mission. In the summer
of 1846, Fremont turned from map-making to grabbing
territory. His chance came when disgruntled American
settlers revolted against Mexican authority in northern California. Carson, as Fremont's right-hand
man, was swept into the drama of the conquest of
California.

Part of the scheme involved seizing San Diego.
But Fremont didn't consult the Pacific Ocean. On
July 26, Fremont's Mountain Men and marines sailed
aboard the sloop *Cyane* from Monterey. Fresh winds
and billowy seas soon had Carson and his Mountaineers heaving over the side. Before sailing they had
astonished the people of Monterey by shooting pesos
at 150 paces; now they lay prostrate on the deck,
seasick. Kit swore he'd never be enticed aboard
another salt-water ship, "not as long as mules has
got backs."

Fortunately for Carson's wobbly-legged men, no
Mexican muskets faced them in San Diego. The marines
marched past friendly faces to hoist the Stars and
Stripes in the plaza. The woebegotten came ashore
later. Kit laid up at the Wrightington family in Old
Town until he regained his land legs. Then he rode

into the backcountry to secure horses for the assault on Los Angeles.

Again, Carson's luck continued. General Jose Castro, the Mexican general guarding Los Angeles, disbanded his army and escaped into Mexico. Fremont's forces, combined with naval units under Commodore Robert F. Stockton, entered the plaza behind a blaring brass band.

Fremont made Kit a lieutenant and ordered him to dash overland to Washington with the electrifying news of California's capitulation. On September 5, Carson led a fifteen-man party out of Los Angeles, through a pass, and out into the desert, riding hell bent for leather. Carson had promised Fremont to reach Washington in 60 days.

On his way to Washington, Carson's luck turned. One morning, they sighted a large Apache village. Carson tactfully told the Apaches they were friends who wished to trade. And after a day of trading, they were allowed through hostile Apache land. But below Socorro on the Rio Grande, Carson ran into a less tractable barrier: General Stephen Watts Kearny and the Army of the West.

Kearny was leading army units westward on a long trek to subdue California and set up a government. Carson's news dismayed Kearny, who ordered three of his five units back. And he dismayed Carson by ordering him to guide the other two units westward. Even after being told that another officer would deliver Fremont's dispatches to Washington, Carson thought of going over the hill at night. Not only had he promised Fremont, but he held high hopes of visiting his wife briefly in Taos on the way.

Carson's temper cooled, and he soon led one hundred men and officers with large, eight-mule wagons and two howitzers across the desert. On November 30, they intercepted a Mexico-bound courier carrying startling dispatches: native Mexicans, Californios,

8

had revolted and recaptured Los Angeles and Santa Barbara from the American occupation forces. The news cheered Kearny and his dragoons; they were itching for a fight.

On December 3, Carson led Kearny's bone-weary men into Warner's Ranch. The long trek, which originated at Fort Leavenworth, Kansas, left the men jaded; their horses and mules were equally exhausted. Several days later, about forty mounted riflemen arrived from Old Town with a message from Commodore Stockton that a "rebel camp" was not far away; Stockton suggested a surprise attack.

At 2 a.m. on December 6, Carson was awakened by the call for boots and saddles. He slapped a saddle on his horse and mounted, his numb hands barely able to hold the reins in the bitter cold. The combined American forces rode some ten miles, topped a rise, and spotted the campfires of the Californios, next to the San Pasqual Indian village.

<h1 style="text-align:center">III</h1>

LOOKING DOWN AT SAN PASQUAL, Kearny told his men to do their duty and ordered a dozen dragoons, under the command of Captain Abraham Johnson and guided by Carson, to lead the attack on the best horses. Early morning darkness and a low fog hung in the valley. The advance force clattered down the hill in two's. Suddenly, Carson's horse stumbled, throwing him headlong, breaking his rifle in two. As the others leaped over him, he escaped being trampled to death by crawling to safety.

With an Indian war whoop, the Americans charged. They saw a line of mounted Californios, dressed in black, ahead of them. They heard cries of "Viva California!" and then bullets whizzing by. Captain Johnson stopped a bullet in the middle of his fore-

head, falling dead. Another dragoon pitched forward
in his saddle, badly wounded. Carson raced a hundred
yards into the battle, where he grabbed the gun and
cartridge box of a fallen American.

Then the second wave of mounted Americans joined
the battle. The Californios suddenly retreated,
racing back into the valley for half a mile. Sensing
victory, the Americans spurred their mounts. But,
riding jaded horses, some half-tamed, and mules, the
Army forces were soon strung out. Andres Pico, commander of the Californios, saw the Americans disorg-
anized and ordered his men to wheel their horses and
attack.

The tide of battle turned. The Californios, su-
perb horsemen on fresh mounts, carried sharp-pointed
lances. The Americans tried to fire their rifles,
which often misfired because of wet cartridges. They
pulled their sabres, but were hopelessly out-reached
by the eight-foot-long lances. Besides, the Californios, many of them *vaqueros*, lassoed the Americans, pulling them to the ground and then piercing
them. The Americans were overwhelmed.

The bloody battle lasted ten minutes. In that
short, seething time—amid screams and curses of the
dying and wounded, amid the snorting and whinnying
of horses and mules—the battle ended. An American
naval officer fired a howitzer, and the threat and
the loud report frightened the Californios. They
fled the battlefield.

As the day dawned, eighteen Americans lay dead in
the San Pasqual Valley. Carson was unscratched.
Nearly every American officer was dead or wounded;
General Kearny barely escaped death, suffering two
bad lance wounds. The dead were lashed to mules.
Carson and others set about making Indian-style
stretchers to move the wounded. Another soldier died
of his wounds, and, at nightfall, nineteen Americans
were buried in a common grave under a willow tree.

10

Next morning, Lieutenant Carson led a battered column. Dragging the wounded on mule-drawn travois slowed them. In the afternoon, as they neared the north shore of what is now Lake Hodges, Pico's lancers tried to encircle the column. Firepower held them off, but then some Californios fired down on the column from a nearby hill. The Americans managed to drive the enemy off the hill and occupied it themselves.

Carson realized their desperate predicament. From the hill, which has come to be known as Mule Hill, he saw Pico's men confidently encircling the Americans. How long could they hold out? They had little food, except they butcher and eat their mules; there was no forage for the animals; no water except what could be found in muddy holes dug in the hillside; half of the men were wounded or sick.

<h2 style="text-align:center">IV</h2>

REINFORCEMENTS FROM Commodore Stockton in Old Town remained the best hope. But three messengers sent the previous day had been captured while trying to return. In a prisoner exchange, however, one messenger related to Kearny that Stockton could not send aid because he lacked sufficient horses. Another message must be sent to Stockton, to make him aware of the seriousness of their situation. Kit Carson, naval Lieutenant Edward Beale, and his Indian orderly volunteered to go.

Carson saw a triple ring of mounted lancers spread around the hill. Unknown to him, Pico had learned of his presence on the hill and warned his men, "Be Watchful! The wolf will escape." The three on the hill got together a little food and water and armed themselves, taking along sharp knives. At nightfall, they slipped out of camp.

With Kit leading, they lowered themselves to the ground to avoid detection against the night sky. In creeping down the granite-strewn hill, the Americans heard their shoes scudding noisily on the granite rock. Stopping, they tucked their shoes under their belts. Crawling again, their progress became painful. Stones cut their flesh. Cactus spines pierced their knees and elbows.

At times, they could reach out in the darkness and touch a lancer's horse. Once, a mounted sentry almost rode over them. They froze. The horse might spot them and snort. To their horror, the sentry dismounted. He ignited a wick, then searched the ground. Carson kicked Beale to lie perfectly still. Kit thought he actually heard Beale's heart pounding.

The sentry lit a cigarette. After a while, he suddenly flipped the cigarette to the ground, near Carson's head. The guard mounted his horse and rode to another sentry. Beale suspected they had been spotted, and the lancer was quietly summoning help. He put his mouth to Carson's ear and whispered:

"We are gone— Let us jump up and fight it out."

"No!" Carson replied. "I have been in worse places than this."

They watched the two sentries conversing in Spanish. Then, to Beale's surprise, they rode off together. After a half mile more of crawling, the Americans had sneaked beyond the third cordon.

Vastly relieved, they stood up and stretched. They picked cactus spines from their tortured flesh. Their smiles were short-lived, however. Carson and Beale had lost their shoes from their belts. The Indian still wore his mocassins. The two lieutenants now faced a march of thirty miles to Old Town— thirty miles of rocks, gravel, and cactus beds— barefooted!

They trudged along as rapidly as they could. Each

step became more painful than the last one for the two, as they left the high ground for the protection of the canyons. The feet of the two officers, cut and bleeding, began to swell. They ran out of water. Their throats were parched. Carson was feverish by nightfall, Beale delirious part of the time.

Then a new danger arose. Surely, the Californios guarded the approaches to Old Town. If apprehended, how could Carson and Beale run on lacerated feet? As they sighted the lights of Old Town, they split up to enhance the odds of one of them getting through. Beale, in the worst shape, hobbled directly toward the lights. His Indian orderly walked toward the coast, then loped southward. Carson chose the longest way, to the south, then circling back on the coast.

The Indian made it first. Taken to Commodore Stockton, he related in Spanish Kearny's deteriorating position. Four hours later, Stockton's guards carried an exhausted Beale into town. He confirmed his orderly's story. Early the next morning, Carson painfully hobbled into town.

Back on the besieged hill the following day, General Kearny gave up on Stockton. He ordered his forces to break out the next morning at sunrise. A few hours before sunrise, however, one of the guards on the hill heard the sound of marching feet coming up the hill. He called out a challenge. Back came the reply, "Americans!" Stockton had sent 100 sailors and 80 marines. Pico's lancers faded into the hills.

The relief party escorted the weary remnants of Kearny's men into Old Town. Lieutenant Beale was incapacitated and did not fully recover for two years. Carson rested, his feet so badly torn and swollen that he could not walk for many days. When he had recovered, he joined the combined Kearny-Stockton forces as chief of scouts.

In January, 1847, they defeated the forces of
General Jose Flores at the San Gabriel River. Carson
was again sent eastward, like a Greek messenger,
with the news of the re-conquest of California. This
time, he saw his family in Taos and President Polk
in Washington. He also rode into American legend.

THE GREAT SCANDAL

A YANKEE SHIP MASTER on the brigantine eyed the channel ahead, observing the mountainous peninsula on his left and the flat island on his right. The year was 1826. Captain Henry Fitch brought the *Marie Ester* into the sleepy port of San Diego. His trader carried a floating store below deck to the little presidio town, cupped in a corner of the bay, which lacked even a single store.

Beneath Captain Fitch's boots lay a whole bazaar of merchandise. Traders like his brought everything from day-to-day items to luxurious fineries. They might carry gun powder and brown sugar, cooking ware and gourd water bottles, silk from China, satin shoes from France, ribbons and bolts of calico for the ladies and gold-embroidered suits and tooled leather saddles for the men.

The handsome ship master came for hides and tallow. Thousands of cattle roamed the hills behind the town. Word would rapidly spread to the ranchos in the back country. Rancheros would bring their hides, their "leather dollars," and bags of tallow to the trader in the bay to barter for the riches in his ship's hold.

Captain Fitch knew, however, that before trade came hospitality, it being an old California custom that pleasure preceded business. So he laid plans to reciprocate for the boundless hospitality to come. The Californios would swarm aboard bringing musicians, dance on his deck, taste the strange delicacies of his cook, and inspect the wondrous cargo below decks.

Later, he would be invited to grand dinners. Flowers everywhere. The gleam of candles on old silver and smiling faces along tables heaped with barbecued beef, roast pig, chili, freshly made tortillas, and wine. And there would be picnics, bull fights, fireworks, and *bailes*.

Bailes would last until daybreak. Everywhere humming guitars, singing violins, clicking castanets, dancing feet. Everybody danced, even elderly ladies. They had their own dance. Balancing a glass of water on their heads, they shuffled their feet and clacked their heels on the adobe floor, without spilling a drop of water. Appreciative guests tossed coins at them.

Romances flourished at these *bailes*. Senoritas prepared perfumed eggs to throw at their suitors. They made a tiny hole in an egg, drained its contents, refilled it with perfume, and sealed it off. When they threw these scented bombs at their unsuspecting beaus, the embarrassed men retaliated by tossing glasses or even buckets of water at their tormentors, chasing the shrieking young ladies out into the moonlight, where the jasmine bloomed.

One day, amidst these festivities, Captain Fitch saw a vision of loveliness. Tall, beautiful, with deep-set eyes and a flawless ivory skin, she enchanted him. She waltzed gracefully. Even though not yet sixteen, she had a free spirit that appealed to him. People called her Josefa.

He learned that she was a Carrillo girl and that Josefa wasn't her real name. She had been bestowed with many, it being the custom: Maria Antonia Natalia Alijia. However, so the story went, three days after her birth, her godmother, Senora Dona Josefa Sal de Mercado, took her to be baptized. Upon returning, Senora Mercado was asked the child's name. Becoming confused with so many names, she replied, "Josefa." The name stuck.

16

Henry Fitch

Josefa, in turn, was flattered by the attention of the tall, American captain. His good manners and handsome presence pleased her. He had a certain air of independence about him. To her, he seemed a man, while the young *caballeros* she knew were overgrown boys. While gay and easy-going, they tended to be shiftless, but Fitch was sober-faced, ambitious, responsible.

However, they were worlds apart. Their language,

nationality, religion, and culture stood between them. But they found that love can bridge any differences. Besides, they shared the common language of love, the language of the eyes.

Still, tall barriers blocked their path. A foreigner, outside the fold of the Catholic Church, could not marry a California senorita. An exemption to the rule could hardly be expected from the Yankee-hating Governor Don Jose Marie Escheandia. This Governor, who chose San Diego as his capital, considered Americans either scoundrels or spies for Spain.

Belles weren't supposed to be friendly with foreigners—a carry-over from the Spanish period, when Spain's fear of land-hungry intruders caused outlanders to be looked on with suspicion. The need for trade alone made the foreigners welcome.

What is more, marriages were arranged by the parents. The father rode out to the ranchos and towns to search for suitable girls for his sons. The youths could indirectly indicate their preference through a useful relative, who would convey the suggestion to the father, but father made the final decision. He ruled the family as an absolute king.

II

THEIR COURTSHIP would be difficult. Captain Fitch, who worked for a Danish shipowner, couldn't remain in San Diego, as he had a schedule of ports to call on. It required courage and patience from Josefa. In love with a protestant Yankee, she must remain steadfast in her vow to wait for him.

During the next three years, Captain Fitch sailed many times in and out of San Diego Bay. In 1827, he stated his honorable intentions to her father, Joaquin, and gave the customary written promise of his desire to wed Josefa. He agreed to convert to Catholicism and to apply for Mexican citizenship.

Finally, everything was ready in the spring of 1829. Arrangements were made. It wouldn't be a church wedding, with the usual elaborate festivities. No, apparently out of fear the governor might step in and ban the marriage, it would be a private ceremony in the Carrillo home.

On April 14, Padre Antonio Menendez, chaplain at the presidio on the hill, accepted Henry Fitch into the fold of the Catholic Church. By baptism, Fitch received the name of Enrique Domingo Fitch. Domingo was Domingo Carrillo, Josefa's uncle, who agreed to be Fitch's godfather.

The following night, the wedding began at the Carrillo adobe. An altar had been prepared in the main room. Close friends and relatives of the family gathered, including Pio Pico. Fitch brought Captain Richard Barry of the *Vulture* to be his best man. Father Menendez, clad in his ecclesiastical vestments, began.

Then it happened. A man suddenly stepped forward. Domingo Carrillo, adjutant to Governor Escheandia, who had only yesterday served as Fitch's godfather, walked up to Padre Menendez. In the name of the governor, he ordered a halt to the proceedings!

Confusion reigned. Father Menendez refused to continue. Fitch was furious, Josefa in tears. What happened next in the uproar of consternation is an open question. One version has the Father advising the distraught couple that there were other Catholic countries where they might be married. And that Josefa looked up into Fitch's gray eyes and said, "Why don't you carry me off, Don Enrique?"

Many years later, Josefa gave her account. She claimed Escheandia was jealous of Fitch, because he wished to win her heart himself. She calculated that his persecution "was only prompted by the wrath which possessed his soul, when he realized that I preferred a rival whom he detested."

In any case, Fitch took Pio Pico aside. He expressed his strong desire to have his rightful aspirations fulfilled and those of Governor Escheandia frustrated. Pico, who understood matters of the heart, advised the captain to return to his ship and prepare to sail. Then, when the night was advanced, to send a boat to shore.

Don Pico went to talk with Josefa. She agreed to elope without telling her parents. Quickly, she gathered some clothing and personal items. She met Pico outside. He helped her mount his horse, and together they rode at top speed to the bayshore.

According to one account, Fitch awaited them there with a boat. Pico bade Josefa farewell, "Goodbye, cousin! May God bless you!"

Turning to Fitch, he pleaded, "And you, Cousin Enrique, take care not to give Josefa cause to repent of having linked her fate with yours."

Solemnly, Fitch responded, "I promise before God and man that as long as I live, Josefa will be happy."

With that, Fitch took her in the boat. They boarded Captain Barry's ship, as Fitch had received instructions to go on the *Vulture* to Valparaiso, Chile, to sell the hides on board. Her anchor raised, the ship stood out to sea on the first breeze.

The next morning, Senor and Senora Carrillo were shocked. Their daughter was gone. The ships of the American captains were gone from the bay. It put Don Carillo in a violent mood. His wife refused to come out of her house. Word spread up the coast as far as Sonoma. The scandal rocked Catholic California. A damnable Yankee had stolen a Spanish belle!

III

THE DAY OF THEIR RETURN dawned ominously. Telltale signs of a storm in the offing filled the heavens. It was July, 1830. As the wind carried the *Leonor* into San Diego Bay, Henry Fitch and Josefa returned. It had been fourteen months since they fled to Valparaiso.

The young lovers had come back. They looked off into the distance where the little adobes lay on the flatland below the presidio and wondered what their reception would be. Would Fitch be attacked for stealing a senorita? Would the governor order them arrested? And how would Josefa's stern father treat them?

Two possessions gave them some confidence: one, a marriage certificate. After a seventy-four-day voyage on the *Vulture,* they had reached Valparaiso, Chile. There they found a parish priest who united them in matrimony in the Catholic tradition. Two, Josefa carried a little bundle. It contained their son, Enrique Eduardo.

The first signs were promising. On learning that the *Leonor* carried Josefa, her mother, Maria, and her sisters came aboard. They were over-joyed to see Josefa well and happy and were delighted with little Enrique. Josefa's father, however, was notable by his absence.

Joaquin Carrillo seethed with hatred for Henry Fitch. Maria told her daughter that he hadn't forgiven her, either. Indeed, he swore he would kill her on sight. Despite the warning, Josefa willingly braved the danger to seek her father's pardon. Leaving the baby with her sisters, she made her way to the family adobe on Wallace Street.

Josefa found the front door half open. On pushing it, she saw her father in the far end of the room.

He sat near a small writing desk, gazing at a musket at his side.

"Father," she declared, "I have returned to San Diego with the object of asking your pardon for having left your home."

Senor Carrillo didn't move. Josefa sensed the storm agitating his soul. His pride had been sorely hurt. The family name had been sullied. His daughter had eloped without his permission. Worse, she was unmarried and unchaperoned. She had defied family, state, and church.

Josefa fell on her knees. From the door, she dragged herself toward him, pleading. She cried she had disobeyed his authority because of the tyranny of the governor. But her father remain motionless. She pulled herself toward the middle of the room, entreating his forgiveness.

Finally, Don Carrillo arose. He turned and went to his daughter and raised he up. "Daughter," he said, "indeed, the fault is not yours, if our governors are despots."

Beside herself with joy, Josefa returned to the door to signal to her mother and other ladies waiting outside. With happy smiles, the women rushed into the home to congratulate Josefa on her father's pardon. That night a grand ball and fireworks celebrated her return.

IV

STORM CLOUDS were still overhead, however. Don Carrillo had not included Henry Fitch in his pardon. The governor hadn't been heard from. And would the church accept their Valparaiso marriage?

Josefa returned to her husband on the *Leonor* for the voyage north. At San Pedro, Fitch received a summons from Padre Jose Sanchez, ecclesiastical judge, to appear before him at the San Gabriel Mission. Certain irregularities of his marriage were to be investigated. Instead of going himself, however, Fitch sent his marriage certificate to Father Sanchez.

Then he sailed north.

Dissatisfied with the wedding document and Fitch's failure to answer the summons in person, Sanchez sent word to Governor Escheandia, at that time in Monterey, to arrest the couple. A Mexican officer boarded the *Leonor* in Monterey Bay and put Fitch in the jail at the presidio. Josefa was placed under house arrest.

Henry Fitch felt bitter. He had converted to the Catholic faith, married Josefa in a Catholic church, and applied for Mexican citizenship. Now, he sat in a jail cell. Moreover, he was losing income; in vain, he demanded compensation from his captors.

The trial took place at the San Gabriel Mission in December. The Fitches faced several charges, including the accusation that Henry had carried off Josefa by force. She silenced that charge. Josefa testified she had gone with Fitch on her free volition; indeed, she suggested the elopement to him.

The church prosecutor cast doubt on the validity of the Valparaiso marriage. Neither of the couple, he pointed out, fulfilled the requirement of being a member of the parish where they were united. Besides, the marriage certificate was blotted with ink and torn.

The captain from New Bedford answered. He pleaded ignorance of the requirement of parish membership. The certificate had been damaged in a shipboard accident, he explained. Ink spilled on the document, and as he hastily snatched the paper, he tore it in places.

Fitch made a closing plea. He said a declaration that his marrige was null and void wouldn't bother him. He simply would marry Josefa again. But nullifying the union would make his son illegitimate, which would be deplorable.

The prosecutor also denounced Governor Escheandia's role. He called the governor's interference a gross infringement on ecclesiastical authority. Declaring the governor a culprit before God's tribunal, he urged his arrest and trial.

On December 28, Padre Sanchez delivered his pronouncement. While decrying Escheandia's conduct, he did not order his arrest and trial. As to the Fitch matrimony, he ruled the prosecutor "has not substantiated his accusations; the marriage at Valparaiso, though not legitimate, is not null and void; I therefore order the parties to be set at liberty and the wife given up to her husband..."

They must do penance, however. For a specific time, they attended church with lighted candles and jointly recited one-third of the rosary of the Holy Virgin. In addition, due to "the great scandal which Don Enrique has caused," he must donate a bell to the church in Los Angeles.

The freed couple settled in San Diego, still under the cloud of the scandal. Don Carrillo still raged at Fitch, taking out his fury on his daughter. He threatened to flog her, telling her she was a common prostitute and her husband a heretic. Fitch, a seafaring man with a salty tongue, wished his father-in-law would go to hell.

In time, the social climate eased. Rancor wore away, as more senoritas married *ojos azules* (blue eyes), as the ladies called the Americans. Besides, as the Yankees began taking over California, the heads of the best families saw advantage in a Yankee son-in-law. Family interest would be served by an American who could help in the new ways of doing business, as well as in legal and political matters.

24

Henry Fitch, who suffered from being ahead of
his time, became a prominent and affluent citizen.
He opened the first store in San Diego and continued
to trade along the coast and with Hawaii. In 1841,
Governor Michaeltorena granted the Fitches a huge
ranch in Sonoma County. During the American Military
occupation in 1846-47, Fitch served as *alcalde*.

Henry and Josefa had nearly twenty years of married life together. Josefa claimed her husband kept
his solemn pledge to Pio Pico on that fateful night
on the beach: "I promise before God and man that as
long as I live Josefa will be happy." She said that
he had never caused her a single sorrow. In the
grand California tradition, they raised a large
family, seven sons and four daughters. And one
daughter they named Josefa.

EL DORADO

IN THE WINTER of 1849, a tall, powerfully-built man, a rifle slung at his back, came out of the desert to Warner's Ranch. The bearded man with wavy locks and the look of a dreamer in his eyes introduced himself to Jonathan Warner, the Ranch owner, as Agoston Haraszthy, a Hungarian. Warner later said he was the most polished figure he had ever beheld at this end of the Santa Fe Trail.

The Hungarian impressed everyone. He conversed brightly in half a dozen languages and played Bach on the piano. At thirty seven, with arched eyebrows and a jet-black beard, Haraszthy seemed the epitome of European culture and mystery. Yet, he was no effete blueblood. A Jefferson democrat, he fiercely believed in equality and would be at ease in the roughest saloon.

He inquired of Warner about California politics and farming. In between resting from his arduous cross-country trek and bathing in the hot springs, he learned of the political situation in the fledgling state. The Magyar's other interest was agriculture. He didn't care a fig for gold prospecting, bringing with him a wagonload of plows, tools, and plants.

His passion was viniculture—wine growing. He came searching for the perfect blend of soil and climate for his vineyard. His dream was to discover the right site and introduce Old World techniques. When he talked of winemaking, his eyes sparkled like the wine he hoped to bottle, communicating a strange excitement to his listeners.

This passion wasn't newborn. Grapes, particularly

Imperial Tokay, had been grown for generations on the Haraszthy estate in Hungary, where Agoston was born near the banks of the Danube on August 30, 1812. Bright and ambitious, he was interested in wine lore and wine chemistry, as well as in politics.

Politics got him into trouble, however. He became the private secretary of the Viceroy of Hungary, Archduke Joseph of Austria. In the late 1830's, rumbles of discontent with Austria's domination of Hungary were heard in the land, and Agoston sympathized with this patriotic movement for autonomy. His involvement aroused the Imperial Austrian wrath. A wary Agoston immigrated to the New World.

He started over in Wisconsin in 1840. He wondered if this new, young land was his El Dorado. He planted vine roots in the cold earth. Soon his boundless energy sprawled in all directions. He founded a town, Haraszthyville (now Saulk City). He sold lots, grew hops, and, with associates, operated a steamboat on the Mississippi, a railroad, a lumberyard, and a chain of grocery stores.

The enterprising Hungarian became an admired figure in prospering Haraszthyville. The tall entrepreneur, wearing his tall silk hat and carrying a cane, commanded respect in the town. Some called him "Count." He preferred, however, to be called Colonel, his rank in the royal Hungarian bodyguard to the Emperor Ferdinand of Austria.

With the discovery of gold in California, however, he thought of moving on. His grapes had not prospered in the harsh Wisconsin climate. He had heard that the Franciscan fathers stamped grapevine cuttings into the rich California soil with their sandals. He could sell his Wisconsin properties at a profit and seek his El Dorado out west.

Driven by ambition, the Colonel packed his family in a covered wagon to join the westward sweep. He brought his father, Charles, his wife, Eleanora, and their six children, Gaza, Attila, Arpad, Bela, Ida, and Otelia. In April, they joined a train of prairie schooners at Independence, Missouri. Agoston became train captain, leading the schooners on horseback on the hazardous, westward wending Santa Fe Trail.

<h2 style="text-align:center">II</h2>

WHEN THE MAGYAR ARISTOCRAT ARRIVED in Old Town in early 1850, he found a wild frontier town. It was awash with raucous gold seekers enroute to "the diggings"— ex-soldiers of the California war on the loose, roustabouts, gamblers, *vaqueros,* toughs. Drinking was the most popular pastime, followed by gambling and fighting, with a few murders tossed in to relieve the tedium.

The town needed a sheriff. Agoston was quite adaptable. He could be a suave diplomat in Emperor Ferdinand's court in Austria, or a pioneer cutting a clearing in the Wisconsin backwoods, or a sheriff in San Diego. In April, he won election as the first sheriff, and, as the town lacked money to pay for a marshall, he assumed that position, too.

Yet, his first love remained growing grapes. Again, he sought the elusive, perfect site for his vineyard. He formed a company that purchased 160 acres in Mission Valley. He got vine roots from Hungary and from French growers in the Los Angeles region. But he had a problem: how to cultivate the soil in such an arid climate. He found the answer by working several weeks with the gardeners at the Mission San Luis Rey.

Law enforcement and growing grapes were hardly sufficient to keep the restless Hungarian occupied. With his talent for promotion, he soon had other businesses going. He ran several with Don Juan Bandini. They had a profitable butcher shop, plus a livery stable and an omnibus. With other investors, he purchased 687 acres to form Middletown, a development that would connect Old Town with New Town to the south on the waterfront.

One project turned into an expensive fiasco for the Colonel. The board of trustees (city council) invited bids for a jail, even though it lacked funds to pay for it. Plans called for a strong cobblestone-and-mortar prison. Agoston submitted a bid of $5,000, while the Israel brothers came up with one for $3,000. The council, with Charles Haraszthy, Agoston's father, as president, awarded him the contract.

While this might smack of nepotism, it proved a financial fiasco to the Colonel. Willing to accept dubious script in lieu of cash, the sheriff-turned-contractor spent his own money. Then disaster. In a heavy rain during construction, the mortar dissolved, leaving a dismal heap of cobblestones. The trustees voted him another $2,000, which it didn't have, to repair the damage. In March, they accepted the jail as completed.

Two problems remained, however. One, he had script, no cash payment. Second, when prisoners began digging holes in the weak mortar to escape, the trustees refused payment in legal tender. The sputtering Hungarian sued in vain to get his money back.

Later that year, the proud Colonel ran for State Assembly. With his fervid oratory and "noble" mannerisms, he won in a tough race. He didn't mind leaving San Diego, as his grape vines had not thrived in Mission Valley. Besides, the stubborn Magyar could introduce legislation to change the form of San Diego's city government, so it could pay off the city's debts—such as to a certain jail contractor!

WHEN THE STATE LEGISLATURE was not in session, the Colonel idled in the bustling city of San Francisco. A magnetic figure in his frock coat and tall silk hat, he blended well into the cosmopolitan setting. When his term in the assembly ended, he decided to seek his El Dorado in the city by the Golden Gate.

He bought two hundred acres near the old Mission Dolores, setting up a nursery and horticultural garden. Down the San Francisco peninsula, he bought more land and planted fruit trees, grain and strawberries, and put in thirty acres of grapes.

As everywhere he tarried, he saw opportunity abound. With the Mother Lode bringing forth an avalanche of gold, he became a partner in the Eureka Gold & Silver Refinery, for among his many skills was a knowledge of metallurgy. In 1854, President Franklin Pierce cast about for a metallurgist to be Assayer for the United States Branch Mint in San Francisco. With millions of dollars of gold to be rolled into strips and stamped into gold coins, he needed an efficient and reliable man. He chose Agoston Haraszthy.

The Colonel got the mint humming. In two years, over $100,000,000 in gold came into the door, to be processed and dropped as bright, yellow coins into iron carts. Inevitable wastage occurred, and Haraszthy warned the superintendent and the treasurer. Still, when a startled bookkeeper reported a hundred and fifty thousand dollar shortage over and above the maximum allowed wastage, eyebrows shot up.

Worse, a confidential investigator of the U. S. Treasury suspected Haraszthy. Looking into his many investments, the investigator suggested he used the gold to further his private affairs. "I consider him an unsafe man," concluded the report, "and would recommend his removal." Haraszthy stoutly maintained his innocence, blaming inefficient machinery for the loss. Amid sensational newspaper accounts, he resigned, and a U. S. grand jury indicted the Colonel for embezzlement.

He never doubted he would be vindicated. He told government investigators the loss had been caused by faulty furnaces. Under forced draft, with the furnaces going night and day, tiny particles had drifted up the mint's flue. They checked it out. The jury agreed on the verdict: "There is no evidence in this case to prove the slightest fraud by the defendant."

IV

IN THE SPRING OF 1857, HARASZTHY stood on the top of a hill north of San Francisco Bay, looking out on a green, hilly landscape. The Indians called it "The Valley of the Moon." He bought 560 acres and named his property *Buena Vista*, Beautiful View. In the Sonoma Valley, he had found his El Dorado.

With his customary energy, he enlarged *Buena Vista* and then enlarged it again. With the aid of his sons and Chinese laborers, he planted thousands upon thousands of rooted twigs, Riesling, Tokay, and Muscat, on sunny slopes. Stone cellars were dug deep into hillsides. With his exacting techniques, *Buena Vista* labels won blue ribbons at state fairs, then world-wide competitions, bringing unprecedented recognition to California wines.

Many honors came to him. The legislature appointed him to a committee to study the California wine industry. He was elected director of the California State Agricultural Society. The governor sent him to Europe to survey winemaking there. In Washington, Secretary of State Seward gave him a note assuring him diplomatic privileges.

He stood at the pinnacle of his spectacular career. Personally, he had the immense satisfaction as a political refugee to return to Europe with United States diplomatic privileges. Economically, his *Buena Vista* set the pace as California jumped into the lead in domestic wine production. Socially, he had the pleasure of union with an old California family in the double wedding of two of his sons to daughters of his neighbor vintner, General M. C. Vallejo.

The Colonel became the prophet of the industry, his *Grape Cultures—Wines and Wine-Making* its bible. He traveled up and down the state in a coach, with grape vines from Europe lashed to its back, demonstrating grape cultivation to growers in secluded valleys. Wherever farmers gathered, he fervently preached the gospel that "California can produce as noble and generous a wine as any in Europe."

The mercurial Colonel, however, was like a bouncing ball; the higher he bounced, the further he fell. It began with the bill for his European junket. The legislature had agreed to his trip, but was under no obligation to pay for it. He brought back a hundred thousand cuttings, three hundred different varieties, and petitioned the legislature for reimbursement, assuring them that the $12,000 requested would "in time be worth as many millions." Surely, a grateful state would reimburse him. It wouldn't.

The worst was yet to come. In enlarging *Buena Vista*, he became heavily mortgaged. How could he diminish his obligations, yet expand production to meet the increased demand for his label? He asked the financial community for advice. The canny William Ralston of the Bank of California had a plan: incorporate *Buena Vista*, with Haraszthy exchanging his equity for stock and continuing as the salaried superintendent of the Buena Vista Vinicultural Society. New capital would allow expansion, and offices would be opened in the East and in Europe. The Colonel agreed.

It didn't work. Friction developed between Haraszthy and Ralston, who didn't understand why the winemaking couldn't be speeded up to increase production. The Colonel, a complete individualist and a man of pride, wasn't going to take such an order. An attempt to make champagne failed. The society failed to pay dividends. Ralston tried to ease Haraszthy out for poor management. The Colonel quit *Buena Vista* in disgust.

For a while, he lived at the Sonoma vineyard owned by his wife and managed by one of his sons. Misfortune continued to hound him. A downturn in the San Francisco stock market diminished the value of his various holdings. A fire raged in the winery. A boiler exploded, and to escape the scalding steam, he jumped from a second-floor window, badly twisting an ankle.

He had reached low ebb. Yet, he was only in his early fifties. An eternal optimist, with the blood of an adventurer, he believed anything was possible —so he sought another El Dorado.

This time, he would be a plantation owner. He would own a hundred thousand acres of the best land in Central America. He would have a mansion again, with servants, and go out among his workers and converse with them in their native language. It would be like in the olden days on his family estate in Hungary, on the banks of the Danube.

It all came true, like a miracle. In three years, the irresistible Colonel sat in baronial splendor in his Hacienda San Antonio in Nicaragua. The charming aristocrat had even talked Nicaraguan officials into granting him a monopoly for the distillation of spirits. He had huge fields of sugar cane and an enormous distillery.

On a humid July morning in 1869, he mounted his horse to search for a saw mill location in the jungle. He found a stream, lined with trees. Tying his horse to a tree, he strolled down to the bank. It seemed a likely site, and he decided to explore the other side of the stream.

A magnolia tree offered an overhanging branch for the crossing. He climbed the tree and worked his way out on the branch. Suddenly, under his weight, the branch gave way beneath him and he plunged into the bubbling water below. The stream was alive with alligators. He had tempted fate for the last time.

Agoston Haraszthy

WITHOUT BENEFIT
OF BLACKSTONE

CHARLES HARASZTHY WAS JUDGE of the San Diego Court of Session in 1850 and 51. Robert Israel, who served as marshall in the court, used to relate an anecdote about the Hungarian judge. In those days, the town and most of its populace were in financial

Charles Haraszthy

straits, so His Honor had to recover all of his court costs from the people who appeared before him.

In suits, the judge could recover court costs from either the plaintiff or the defendant. In those impoverished times, however, the plaintiffs were usually destitute. They sued a well-off person for money supposedly owed them, hoping to come into a few dollars. And they had the help of His Honor, who figured he could only recover court costs out of the moneyed defendants.

"Ve must gif de shudgment to de man vat gifs us de pizness," declared Judge Haraszthy. In short, he gave the award to the plaintiff, completely ignoring the merits of the case. This startling and expedient way of deciding cases worked. That is, until the Morales-Couts case.

A man named Morales came to Marshall Israel to sue Blount Couts, son of a wealthy ranchero. The marshall told Morales that his fee for serving the summons and collecting the award would be fifteen dollars. "But I don't have any money," said Morales. All right, the marshal replied; he would agree to take the fee out of the award. So the marshall served Couts the summons.

A furious Couts appeared on the date of the trial, and everything went awry. Couts not only denied that he owed Morales anything, but maintained that, in reality, Morales owed him money. Couts set about to question Morales.

"Didn't I pay you so much on such and such a date?"

"Yes, sir, so you did," admitted the honest Morales.

Marshall Israel, visualizing his fifteen dollars flying out the window, cautioned Morales. "Shut up, you fool, he'll have you owing him money in a minute."

"Well, but, senor, it is true," replied the

Mexican.

Couts kept to his hard questioning. Finally, the hapless Morales admitted that he actually owed the defendant twenty-five cents.

At which point, the befuddled judge asked the marshall. "Vell, vat ve goin' to do now?"

"Well," replied Israel, "there is nothing I can see to do except render judgment."

"Vell," said the judge, turning to Couts, "I shall gif shudgment against you for twenty-five cents."

Couts hotly retorted, "I'll be damned if I'll pay it; the man has acknowledged himself indebted to me!" With that, he got up and left the court.

"Vell, vat ve goin' to do now?" the exasperated judge asked the marshall.

"Well, enter judgment against this Mexican for twenty-five cents."

"Vell," replied the judge, "but dis man he got no money. Ve must gif de shudgment to de man vat gifs us de pizness."

LATER, BLOUNT COUTS SOUGHT REVENGE on Morales. He knew the Mexican possessed a fine horse, saddle, and bridle in his corral. Couts went to the sheriff, who happened to be another Hungarian, to get an attachment on Morales's personal property.

Marshall Israel, however, caught wind of this. He rushed to find Morales to warn him. He found him drinking in a *cantina*. Morales asked the marshall what he should do. "Sell the horse, saddle, and bridle quickly," Israel urged.

"Well, why don't you buy them?" asked Morales.

"I don't want them, but to keep them from being seized, I will take them for sixty-five dollars and pay you fifty dollars, if you allow for the fifteen dollars I was to have out of the case."

Morales accepted the offer. The bartender made

out a bill of sale, the Mexican put his mark to it,
and Israel paid him fifty dollars. Just as the marshall tucked the bill of sale into his pocket, in
strode the sheriff with an attachment in his hand.

The sheriff asked the marshall if Morales had a
horse, saddle, and bridle.

"No," answered Israel.

"Well, he did have."

"Yes, but he has none now. He has just sold
them," replied the marshall, whipping out the bill
of sale.

Bristling with anger, the sheriff threw the bill
of sale on the floor and snorted that this was "one
of your damn Yankee tricks."

The sheriff hated the marshall after that—which
might explain why San Diego sheriffs and marshalls
have been feuding ever since.

THE UPRISING OF ANTONIO GARRA

ON THE MORNING of July 6, 1847, Chief Antonio Garra led some eighty Cupeno Indians into Los Angeles. The resident Californios were startled. The boldness of the entry stunned them, raising the ugly specter of a bloody Indian raid. Their fright was heightened by a rumor that the Indians, camped temporarily on the far side of the river, had large numbers of rifles, pistols, and lances.

Chief Garra, however, came on a mission of peace. Leader of the Cupenos who lived about Warner's Rancho, he came to talk with the American military authorities. He thought the Americans, who had recently captured California from Mexico, would treat the Indians better than the Californios had. The previous December, General Stephen Kearny had promised Garra that the Indians would be well treated if they kept the peace and worked hard.

At 10 a.m., Garra had the Indians assembled before the Army barracks. He spoke to Lieutenant J. D. Stevenson, who raised the question of Indian thievery. They admitted to cattle stealing, but convinced Stevenson they were not responsible for the robbery of Mission San Luis Rey. Chief Garra suggested an Indian agent be appointed over them. The agent, however, should be an American, not a Californio.

Lieutenant Stevenson agreed. He promised to appoint an American Indian agent within six weeks. With that, Garra led his Cupenos back to their green valley in San Diego County, where the men dispersed to their villages around Warner Springs.

Garra returned to his village of Kupa (Agua Caliente). There, he lived with his Mission wife and his son, who had the same name as his father, in a house that was large, compared to the thatched huts of his followers. The chief owned many cattle and horses, and, it is said, books.

He had received his education at the Mission San Luis Rey, where he was baptized and learned to read and write Spanish. The padres had taught him his catechism, and, with the other neophytes, he had received instruction in planting crops and caring for livestock. But the missions had been abandoned; the padres had gone away.

Now, Garra saw the Anglos coming. From his village on the road from the Colorado River to Los Angeles, he watched the Americans in small parties and large immigration wagon trains. After the discovery of gold in 1848, the stream of newcomers became a flash flood. He began to fear this torrent of Americans endangered the Indians.

At first, Garra had welcomed the foreigners. In early December, 1846, Cupeno women had ground flour for General Kearny's weary dragoons at Warner's. The following month, Chief Garra and ten of his men led the Mormon Battalion into the upper reaches of the Temecula Valley. Like other Indians, he thought the Americans would treat them better than the Californios had.

By the summer of 1851, however, he had been disillusioned by the Anglos. Garra no longer trusted their word. The promise of General Kearny wasn't kept. The Indian sub-agent appointed by Lieutenant Stevenson four years before had failed to alleviate the problems of Garra's people.

In June, Chief Garra learned that Indian Commissioner George W. Barbour was coming to negotiate with the Indians of San Bernardino and San Diego County. The Indians were anxious for a treaty, as they had heard that northern California Indians had

40

been granted land and had been given food and farm implements. The southern California Indians arrived at the designated meeting place, waited five days, and angrily departed. Barbour didn't appear.

Indian taxation also made Garra furious. In 1850, Sheriff Agoston Haraszthy levied county taxes on the Cupenos, Luisenos, and Dieguenos, collecting six hundred dollars. The following year, he again rode out into Indian country to assess their cattle, horses, sheep, and hogs.

Yet, that summer, Garra also received a command not to pay the tax. General Joshua Bean, commander of the militia for the southern part of the state, forbade the Indians of San Diego County to pay. Nonetheless, Sheriff Haraszthy told Garra and the other chiefs that, unless they paid the levied tax, he would return and confiscate their herds.

This was the last straw. Although he sent his son to Old Town to pay part of the assessment in cash, the more he thought about it, the madder he got. Indians received no protection in return, had no representation, and were denied both property and civil rights. Indeed, an Indian could be shot, simply for getting ahead of a white man.

II

CHIEF GARRA DECIDED—the white foreigner must go.

Moreover, he believed the Indians could defeat the Anglos. While their numbers had increased, the Americans were still thinly spread out in southern California. They had numbers only in several poorly defended coastal towns. With their vast numerical superiority, the Indians could prevail by coordinated attacks. Besides, he figured, the Californios would join the Indians to get rid of the Anglos.

So he devised a war plan. First, the river Indi-

ans would attack Camp Independence on the Colorado
River, to seize arms and prevent the deployment of
Army units from there to defend the towns on the
coast. Then, the Tularenos would attack Santa Barbara; the Cahuillas and Cupenos, Los Angeles; and the
Quechans (Yumas), San Diego. Only Americans were to
be killed.

Next, Garra embarked on his most critical task—
unifying the diverse and jealous Indian societies.
He told the Indians not to fear the American bullets; he would turn them to water. He gave a feast
for Cahuilla leaders. He communicated with leaders
at San Luis Rey, Santa Isabel, San Pasqual, and
Temecula. He sent runners as far south as Baja California and as far north as central California.

All through the summer and fall of 1851, he tried
to forge an Indian alliance. He had mixed results.
Most Luisenos chose not to fight the Americans. The
Tularenos in Central California negotiated a treaty
with Commissioner Barbour and refused to break it.
The top chieftain of the Cahuillas, Juan Antonio,
picked the path of cooperation over that of resistance.

Yet, other Indians flocked to Garra's banner. He
won over the river Indians, the Quechans, Cocopas,
and probably the Kamias, led by the fierce Geronimo.
Some of the lesser Cahuilla chiefs chose to fight
the palefaces. In addition, the Baja California Indians were ready to revolt.

In the winter, Garra rode across the desert to
the Colorado River to start the uprising. He considered the ferry crossing of the river a vital link,
because it was bringing supplies and immigrants into
southern California. Besides cutting this link, he
urged the river Indians to knock out the nearby
military garrison, Camp Independence.

On November 11, seven sheepmen and some fifteen
hundred sheep crossed the Colorado. Quechans and

Cocopas surrounded the shepherds and demanded their provisions and blankets. A gunfight ensued in which five sheepmen and seven Indians were killed.

A few hours later, Indians surrounded Camp Independence. Saying they came to trade, they offered one horse for every American blanket. The commanding officer, thinking these terms too good to be true, suspected a ploy to gain entrance. He ordered the Indians to disperse.

They refused. The officer placed his twelve-pound howitzer in position to cover the camp entrance. The dismayed Indians retreated. For two successive nights, they rained arrows on the garrison, but both the alertness of the soldiers inside and the threat of the howitzer kept the Indians at bay.

While they could besiege the camp, the Indians found a direct attack impossible. In the meantime, a dispute broke out between the Quechans and the Cocopas over the division of the captured sheep. Turning bitter, the Quechans decided they had had enough of the war.

Garra rode across the desert with a heavy heart. He had failed to overrun Camp Independence, his first objective. Worse, he had lost the cooperation of the Quechans, who were to attack San Diego. He faced the grim reality that his uprising was falling apart. Knowing the Americans would strike back, he must have suffered second thoughts about the wisdom of the revolt.

When he reached Los Coyotes Canyon, he had alarming news. An attack on Warner's Rancho was imminent. He tried to talk the Cahuilla leaders out of the raid, but he became ill and failed. This wasn't in his war plan, and now he would be blamed for it.

The results distressed him. Juan "Long John" Warner of Warner's Rancho escaped the attack, killing two Indians. The Cahuillas ransacked Warner's house and ran off his cattle. Another Indian party, led by

Garra's son, found four American invalids who had come to the hot springs, unaware of the uprising. They were killed and their possessions divided.

These events deeply afflicted Garra. Indeed, his despondency reduced him to a stony silence. He had lost control over the revolt. His war plans had quickly degenerated into sporadic raids of revenge and plunder. Yet, he had started a war. His one hope lay in gaining more allies.

He tried to involve the Californios. He sent a letter to the prominent Jose Antonio Estudillo. "Now the blow is struck," he wrote. "If I have life I will go and help you, because all the Indians are invited in all parts, and it is possible that the San Bernardinos (Cahuillas) are now rising..."

Again, he tried to win the powerful Chief Juan Antonio to his banner. He warned Antonio that this was the Indians' last chance. "If we lose this war, all will be lost—the world. If we gain this war, then it is forever; never will it stop; it is for the whole of life."

In reply, Chief Antonio asked for a meeting. Would Chief Garra meet with him at the desert village of Razon? Garra didn't want to go, probably suspecting a trap. But his Cahuilla friends at Los Coyotes encouraged him to go. Finally, he went, perhaps realizing that if he failed to win over Antonio, it was all over anyway.

It was a trap. Antonio, likely incensed that Garra had won over some of his Cahuillas, decided to capture Garra. At Razon, he had him seized, stripped of his clothing, and taken to the village, Sahatapa. There, for gifts and to curry favor with the American forces, Antonio turned Garra over to General Joshua Bean.

WITH HIS CAPTURE, Garra knew all was lost. His vision of an Indian alliance to rid southern California of the white foreigner had turned to ashes. Resistance now only meant more needless bloodshed. He urged his son to surrender, and young Garra obeyed.

Garra was taken to Old Town for a court martial, and his son to Chino. Both were charged with treason, murder, and robbery. Young Garra confessed to being a member of the party that killed three of the four American invalids and to stealing at the Warner Rancho. The military tribunal convicted him of all charges, and he was shot to death on the morning of December 27.

On January 9, 1852, the military court opened the trial of Chief Garra. He acknowledged responsibility only for the killing of the American sheepherders, although he claimed he had tried to prevent that incident. He stated he opposed the raid at Warner's, but was too ill to prevent it.

His defense counsel insisted that Garra couldn't be guilty of treason. He argued that, not having sworn allegiance to the United States, he could not have committed treason. Besides, as an Indian chief, he had a right to declare war. The court accepted these arguments, but convicted him of murder and theft and ordered him executed that same afternoon.

At four-thirty, the firing squad paraded before his cell. The provost marshall told the old chief his hour had come. Garra was calm. The second man in his cell, Father Juan Holbein, considered Garra's indifference unbecoming; he should be contrite, beseeching the Almighty for forgiveness.

"What is the use?" Garra replied. "That is of no account."

The procession to the cemetery commenced. Still bothered that the condemned man didn't pray, Holbein stopped, insisting that Garra supplicate. To placate the aging priest, Garra began to pray while Holbein recited Latin.

Then, to the amazement of the firing squad, they heard Chief Garra correcting Holbein's Latin! This dispute over Latin continued until they reached a freshly-dug grave at the Catholic cemetery.

There, before a large crowd of Old Towners and Indians that had gathered in the chill of the late January afternoon, a new quarrel erupted. Father Holbein asked Garra to seek a pardon for his sins from those assembled. Garra refused. Yet, after repeated commands and entreaties, he agreed.

Lifting his eyes, he said in a loud and clear voice, but with a contemptuous smile, "Gentlemen, I ask your pardon for all my offenses and expect yours in return."

One of the executioners stepped forward to tie a handkerchief over the prisoner's eyes. Garra laughingly refused. Again, Holbein insisted. The chieftain yielded and was blindfolded. The priest stepped aside.

Chief Garra kneeled before his grave. At the command of "Ready," the ten men raised their rifles to their shoulders. "Aim." They stared down the sights of their gun barrels at Antonio Garra's chest.

"Fire." Dogs howled at the sharp noise. The sun lingered a last moment on the crest of Point Loma, as church bells chimed vespers. Somehow, there was no rejoicing in Old Town that night.

HIGH FINANCE IN
THE OLD WEST

PHILIP CROSTHWAITE, a big, jovial, bewhiskered Irishman, served as county treasurer in the 1850-1851 term. Juan Bandini had been elected treasurer in the first county election, but chose not to serve. Crosthwaite replaced him. Ephraim Morse, the New England merchant, delighted in spinning this tale about Crosthwaite in the early days when San Diego was dirt poor.

Crosthwaite's duties included gathering county taxes. He also had to deliver revenues in person to the State Treasurer at the capital by a certain settlement date. The treasurer, in turn, would compensate Crosthwaite for his travel expenses.

The big Irishman dutifully saddled his horse and rode out into the back country. Although San Diego county then covered much of Southern California, it consisted of vast stretches of land with a few scattered ranchos.

He collected several thousand dollars. But most of this was earmarked for county officials' salaries. As the settlement day with the State Treasurer neared, he tossed the balance in his satchel, along with the proverbial extra shirt and Colt pistol. Crosthwaite then boarded a sidewheeler heading north.

Arriving at the capital, Crosthwaite turned the San Diego county tax receipts over to the State Treasurer. The amount came to a little over two hundred dollars. As the law stipulated, the State Treasurer then handed Crosthwaite compensation for his travel expenses. This came to three hundred dollars.

Crosthwaite was pleasantly surprised by this extraordinary money exchange. He would actually be walking out of the State Treasurer's office with more money than he entered with. And the money would be his, not the county's!

The State Treasurer, on the other hand, was struck dumb by this odd transaction. He recovered his cool tongue, however, to make a suggestion: Under similar circumstances next year, it would be more financially satisfactory to the State of California if Crosthwaite turned embezzler and absconded with the county taxes!

Philip Crosthwaite

48

ROY BEAN'S DUEL
ON HORSEBACK

IN 1849, ROY BEAN rode his weary horse into the dusty presidio town of San Diego. For the feisty Roy, it had been another harrowing escape—this time from two raging mobs in Mexico. His folks back in the Kentucky hills would be pleased, for the cocky youth followed family tradition. He was a fighter.

Roy got the idea early. Whenever his poor but proud family gathered with other Beans, the talk sooner or later turned to the exploits of the tribe. Little Roy heard his kin had fought in the Revolutionary War, the War of 1812, and in Indian campaigns. He knew the Beans weren't the sort to take guff from anybody. Indeed, nobody pushed a Bean around and lived to brag about it.

He grew up in the green hills of Kentucky, where he got a sound frontier education. The family wasn't much for book learning, but Roy caught on to reading and writing a bit, even though it was painfully slow for him. But he picked up what was important: how to fell a tree, shoot a deer, butcher a hog, swap horses, drink whiskey, fight a man, and sweet-talk a girl.

Roy grew into a sturdy mountain lad. Like his two older brothers, Joshua and Sam, he was stocky and muscular. He had a fair complexion, with black, silky hair. Dressed up, he made quite a handsome beau.

He caught the Western fever from his brothers. Joshua took off for "Californy." Sam struck out for what he thought would be high adventure and romance. At about sixteen, Roy couldn't stand it any longer at home. He joined up with a party going down the river to New Orleans. They had a batch of slaves to sell.

But he had a twin named trouble. With an instinctive urge to do as he pleased, regardless of the consequences, he easily found his way into a peck of trouble. He did so on this first trek down the river. Roy never talked about this episode. Whatever it was, he got out of the jam by escaping home to the hills of Kentucky.

In the dog days of 1847, brother Sam knocked at the Beans' rough plank door. Delighted to have him home, the family asked him where he had been.

"Fightin' the Mexicans," said a tuckered-out Sam. "I just got my discharge at New Orleans the end of June, and I ain't fixin' to fight any more war."

In the shade that summer, Roy heard tell of Sam's doings. He heard how Sam nearly died of starvation in the desert and of his hardships in the Mexican War. But he also learned of a new world, a world of great deserts and tall mountains, of fierce Indians and beautiful women. Roy's eyes grew bigger and bigger.

In the spring of 1848, Roy and Sam left for Independence, Missouri. Sam had an idea to make money. He bought mules, a wagon, supplies, and a stock of trading goods at Independence. Then the Bean brothers joined a wagon train, which was soon snaking across the Midwestern plains. However, before they reached Santa Fe in New Mexico Territory, Sam got to thinking the pickings might be better further south.

So they took a detour and finally pitched camp in Chihuahua, Mexico. Sam hit it right. The Mexicans were hungry for American goods. The brothers set up a trading post and sold everything they could lay their hands on, including whiskey. With a grin, the natives called them *Los Frijoles*.

Roy never had it so good. A poor nobody in Kentucky, in Chihuahua, he had money and was a somebody: an American and a merchant. Besides, he took to the leisurely Mexican way of life. He developed a taste for the fiery tequila. He delighted in chili con carne with liver.

Furthermore, Roy loved the pomp he found in Mexico. He liked the fineries the Mexican gentlemen wore at fiestas. And he picked up the courtly manners of the *caballeros*. It tickled him to dress up in a Mexican costume and practice Spanish manners with the senoritas.

But with him, nothing good ever lasted long. In 1849, as Roy told the story, a big Mexican badman, feeling his liquor, decided to clean the gringos out of Chihuahua.

The *hombre* started with Roy. The desperado entered the Bean *tienda* and commenced to wreck the place. Sam was away in Santa Fe at the time. Roy ordered the man out. With drawn knife, the bully advanced toward the American. Roy warned him again to stand back. But he kept coming, leering and waving his knife. When he got within a few feet, Roy fired a bullet between the badman's eyes.

News of the murder spread like quicksilver. Mexicans gathered in litle clots in the street. They joined other clots, and a mob formed. A few inflammatory words sounded the tocsin. The mob moved toward the Bean trading post, bent on lynching Roy Bean. But before they reached the store, Roy grabbed what money he could and sneaked out of town.

He fled to Jesus Maria in the northeast corner of Sonora. But the news beat him there. A hostile reception committee prepared a welcome. The American merchants in the mining town rallied to Bean's defense. A battle broke out. The enraged Mexicans turned on the gringos, sacking their *tiendas* and driving them out of town. Bean escaped again.

Roy Bean

II

IN SAN DIEGO, Roy sought out his oldest brother, Joshua. He knew his brother had set out for California with American soldiers three years earlier. And he believed Joshua had settled in San Diego. Roy made inquiries. Did anybody know where he could find Joshua Bean?

Bean? Bean! Why, senor, everybody knows Bean, came the reply; Bean is the *alcalde*. Roy thought that was rich. His own brother, political boss of the place! He saw happy days ahead.

Roy was right. Pleased to see him, Joshua practically gave him the keys to the town. Doors opened, and smiling faces greeted him. As the brother of the *alcalde*, he got invited to the *bailes* to dance with the pretty senoritas. Soon, he swaggered about town, gambling on cock fights and horse races.

In 1850, Roy assumed even greater airs. In that year, the American form of government replaced the Mexican, and his popular brother became the first mayor of San Diego. What is more, the State Legislature appointed Joshua Bean a Major General in the State Militia.

Roy was in his element. Dressed in the gay trappings of a *caballero*, the young blood cut a dashing figure. His smattering of Spanish and the courtly manners he picked up in Chihuahua made him irresistible to the senoritas.

The rake's progress didn't go unchallenged. Jealous young blades in town resented his success at love-making. They had heard he had killed a Mexican badman. Still, they were eager to find a challenger to knock him down a notch. They found their man. They goaded a Scotsman named John Collins into challenging Roy.

Their opportunity came in February, 1852. Roy had lost the protection of his benefactor, Joshua Bean, who had pulled up stakes and moved north in 1851. One day, a number of young bucks drinking in a *cantina* surrounded Roy. They directed the banter to shooting ability, and Roy obligingly bragged about his marksmanship.

"Collins here is a crack shot," one of them boasted. "Why don't you and him have a contest?"

Roy may have thought this just whiskey talk. But Collins's supporters insisted on a match to decide the best marksman. Roy finally agreed. "All right, but what 'll we shoot at?"

Collins had an answer. "Let's fire at a target from a moving horse."

Roy sized up Collins. "I'll tell you what we ought to do," he said with a crooked grin. "You shoot at me, and I'll shoot at you."

Collins's face dropped. This wasn't what he had in mind. But he couldn't back down now. "All right," he replied, "we'll do it that way."

The drowsy village awoke with a start. A gunfight on horseback! Villagers knew of sword and pistol duels, but who had seen a pistol duel from horses? Merchants told their customers. The word spread to the ranchos. Excitement mounted for the new sporting event.

But would Sheriff Agoston Haraszthy permit a blazing gun battle in the streets? Old Towners wondered. Certainly, the Spanish tradition and even the Hungarian customs of Haraszthy honored dueling. But American courts frowned on it. Surprisingly, the sheriff decided to allow the duel, although he is said to have warned, "If any spectators get shot, I'll have to arrest the duelist responsible."

Finally, February 24, 1852, dawned bright and clear. Shrove Tuesday, the last day of Mardi Gras. A festive air permeated the crowd. Rancheros came in by horse and *carreta*. The *cantinas* and stores would do well this day.

The spectators gathered about the roped-off street. Senoritas in bright *mantillas* lined the street to cheer for the dashing Senor Bean. Supporters of the Scotsman arrived to see their man give this cock-of-the-walk his come-uppance.

Cheers rose for the handsome Roy Bean. He wore his *caballero* finery: tight-fitting trousers of black velvet, embroidered cutaway jacket, expensive boots and a flat-crowned, wide-brimmed hat. He sat confidently astride his sleek roan, emblazoned with a silver-studded saddle and bridle.

54

John Collins also received applause as he rode into the arena. Although dour-faced, the Scotsman tried to appear nonchalant and assured as he awaited the signal to begin. But he sat tense in the saddle.

Sherrif Haraszthy gave the signal. His warning about stray shots hitting spectators forced the duelists to maneuver their horses frantically. Each sought the protection of onlookers to his back, while trying to get his opponent before an open area where spectators were not allowed to gather.

The nervous Collins fired first. From some distance, he triggered a shot. He missed. As they drew near, Bean took dead aim at the Scot's forehead. He pulled the trigger. The hammer snapped harmlessly.

They continued jockeying for position. Bean placed himself with his back to the crowd, forcing the Scotsman into the open area. Realizing his vulnerability, Collins spurred his horse to race by the Kentuckian.

Bean re-cocked his pistol. As Collins dashed by, Bean wheeled his horse, aimed, and fired. The bullet clipped the Scot in the leg. Re-cocking again, Bean got off another shot. This one struck Collins's horse.

The mount and Collins collapsed in a heap. The crowd cheered wildly for the victory of Roy Bean. Somebody rushed to Collins's side. His wound proved superficial, but his horse was fatally wounded.

Out of the crowd stepped the tall Hungarian sheriff. To the amazement of Bean and Collins, Haraszthy announced they were both under arrest. He marched them down San Diego Avenue to the cobblestone-and-mortar jail.

That afternoon, they were led to court. Charges were set as assault with intent to commit murder. Collins faced an additional charge of challenging Bean to a duel and Bean, of accepting. Bail was put at $1,000 each. The trial would be in a month.

Bean didn't suffer pangs of loneliness in jail.
Adoring senoritas brought him baskets and shawl-
bundles of food—cold chicken, tamales, enchiladas,
dulces, wine, and cigars, even flowers to brighten
his drab jail cell. They vied for position at the
grating to hand gifts to their American hero.

Yet, Roy wasn't one to be fenced in. Besides, he
had a hankering to visit his brother Josh, who operated the Headquarters Saloon at San Gabriel. He
found a way. The San Diego *Herald* reported, "Bean
having broke jail and escaped..."

Exactly how he performed the trick is not known.
Afterwards, Bean gallantly denied the ladies slipped
him any sort of contraband, like a file in a tamale.
If he didn't cut through the bars, however, he
gouged a big enough hole in a wall to crawl through.
Roy claimed no tools were needed to burrow through a
wall of inferior mortar.

But he did have outside help. When he broke out,
there behind the jail stood his roan. Fully capari-
soned, his mount carried his holster and pistol,
slung at the pommel. To complete his escapade, Roy
Bean simply jumped on his horse and hied north.

"THE BEST LAID PLANS.."

IN DECEMBER 1850, a large man appeared on San Diego Avenue, passing out a prospectus for a newspaper. Indeed, the man in the black satin suit and sash tie was a giant. Six feet, six and a half inches tall, the mysterious stranger possessed the broad shoulders and muscular figure of a Hercules. He said his name was Ames, John Judson Ames, and he hailed originally from a town in Maine, near the Canadian border.

Old Towners scratched their heads. A newspaper in their little village? It hardly seemed worthwhile. Everyone knew the local news long before a weekly could get around to printing it. Out-of-town news? Well, that came from newspapers dropped by coastal steamers. Anyone could pick up the news without waiting for the local paper to reprint it.

Besides, his readership couldn't be over a few hundred. Only about a third of the town's six hundred odd inhabitants read English. Plus, there was a small enclave of Americans at the fledgling village three miles to the south, New Town. But certainly the handful of businesses and few professional men were insufficient advertisers. They and his subscribers hardly could keep Ames's creditors in abeyance and pay his lodging and victuals.

But Judson Ames appeared cheerfully unconcerned about making a go of it. He seemed to know something the local people didn't. With his big man's charm, he walked about Old Town and New Town, introducing himself and handing out his prospectus. He took subscriptions at ten dollars a year and arranged advertising contracts.

Ames then departed. He reappeared in the spring of the following year with his printing equipment. He set up his Washington press and type cases above a store on Fourth Avenue in New Town. There he put out Volume I, Number 1, of the San Diego *Herald*, dated Thursday, May 29, 1851.

Subscribers saw a four-page newspaper. Front page "news" consisted of a list of 320 unclaimed letters at the post office. Readers noticed a number of news items and two columns of local advertising. But one thing dumbfounded them: many columns of advertising — from San Francisco!

The riddle of Ames deepened. Why so many advertisements from San Francisco? And why so many frequent and unexplained absences from town? Where did he go and what did he do? One cynical rumor had him sampling the fleshpots of San Francisco. Nobody seemed to know what he did.

During these sojourns, Ames left his foreman in charge. Occasionally, he hired an interim editor. One of these editors pro-tem, George Derby, put the riddle into verse:

> *There was a man whose name was Ames,*
> *His aims were aims of mystery;*
> *His story odd, I think by —,*
> *Would make a famous history.*

II

JOHN JUDSON AMES was born in Calasis, Maine, on May 18, 1821. His father owned a shipbuilding firm. At first, young Ames's world was small. There was his mother's kitchen and, later, his father's shipyard. He shot up into a tall and strong Yankee, energetic and ambitious.

When Ames was sixteen, his father pulled him aside. "Jud, you are old enough to take care of yourself, and I think there is enough of the Yankee in you to insure your success," he said. "Be industrious— practice economy— shun wine and women—"

His father promised to help him get started on his own.

But Jud had a bad beginning. In the early 1840's, he sailed before the mast as a second mate on one of his father's ships, bound for Liverpool. Nearing the end of the return voyage, he ran into trouble. While the crew moored the ship to a Boston wharf, runners from a lodging house jumped aboard and tried to lure the crew ashore with promises of whiskey and women.

Young Ames protested. If they were patient until the ship had been secured and cleaned, he told the runners, the crew could go where they pleased. The toughs were contemptuous of the second mate. An argument broke out, and one struck Jud on the chest. Big Jud hit back with what he thought a light blow, and, to his horror, the runner fell dead at his feet.

Boston police arrested Ames. Brought to trial for manslaughter, he heard the other runners swear hard against him. Convicted, he received a long prison sentence. Then, with a bleak future before him, a political intervention saved him from many years in the Leverett Street Jail. President John Tyler interested himself in the case. Understanding the circumstances of the fracas, he gave Jud a presidential pardon.

Enormously relieved, young Ames started over. First, he returned to school to complete his education. Then, being of a literary bent, he worked as a reporter. In 1848, he took off for Baton Rouge, Louisiana, where he founded a paper called the *Dime Catcher*. With a budding interest in politics, he editorially supported the presidential candidacy of General Zachary Taylor.

When the cry of gold swept the world, his dreams

John Judson Ames

turned to California. He struck off for El Dorado, landing in San Francisco in 1849. He found it a wild, hectic place. A medley of races had gathered, speaking many tongues, but all bent on getting rich quickly. Money changed hands rapidly. Miners made fortunes by day and lost them by night at the gambling tables. Schemes to get rich were hatched in every saloon.

Jud had a more immediate problem— he was penniless. But, with his entrepreneurial zeal, he borrowed a handcart and started a business hauling baggage for incoming gold-seekers. Soon, he had coins jingling in his pockets. Genial and generous,

60

Ames made friends easily. He met people at Masonic Lodge meetings and while carousing at Barry and Patten's.

Thus he met one man who changed his life. In this intoxicating atmosphere, he became acquainted with William Gwin, one of California's first two United States Senators. Senator Gwin, a transplanted Tennesseean, had elaborate plans to extend the influence of the South into the Pacific area. And these plans called for a political-minded publisher to found a newspaper in San Diego. To Ames, it seemed his El Dorado.

A transcontinental railroad lay at the heart of Gwin's schemes. Dixieland and an obscure little village named San Diego would be linked along the 32nd parallel. Iron monsters would carry Southern trade to San Diego Bay for distribution to the Pacific Basin. And settlers from Dixie would make Southern California a bastion of Southern sympathizers.

This was only the beginning. Gwin planned to split California into two states. Southern California would enjoy the political plums of having its own congressmen, two Senators, its own Governor, and a state legislature. And the capital of this new state? San Diego!

Nor was this all. American military adventurers, known as filibusters, would seize foreign territory for annexation as slave states to the United States. These filibusters had their eyes peeled on Lower California. With a railroad and its magnificient bay, San Diego would be a trade center to the South.

A madman's dream? No, Ames knew it was all possible. A transcontinental railroad was inevitable. Divergent interests of northern and southern California would lead to friction and agitation to divide the state. Manifest Destiny, the doctrine of an imperial America, was in the air. A few bold men could change the borders of the United States. Had not Sam Houston and a few ragged men beaten Santa Ana, and prepared the way for the annexation of Texas?

Jud Ames fitted into these grandiose plans as publisher in the important-city-to-be, San Diego. The paper would rally San Diego support for the railway, for splitting the state, and for Gwin's imperialist schemes.

In return, Ames would become political boss of the southern end of the state. For securing Democratic majorities in his district, he could expect emoluments from party bigwigs. Furthermore, San Francisco merchants, paying their "dues" to the party machine, would fill half of Ames's newspaper with advertisements.

Ames couldn't turn it down.

III

THE BIG MAN ARRIVED on the lonely shores of San Diego in December, 1850. Intoxicated with Gwin's vision of a city to rival San Francisco, he could but smile at this somnolent village of manana. He knew the curtain was about to go up on its magnificient future. Meantime, he passed out his prospectus, sold subscriptions and advertising contracts.

Then he boarded a steamer and went to New Orleans to secure and pack his Washington press and type cases for the return trip. It wasn't easy. In recrossing the Isthmus of Panama, his boat sank, dropping his printing equipment into the shallow Chagres River. His boatmen fished out some of the lighter equipment, but couldn't budge a four-hundred-pound casting from the press. Growing impatient, the burley Ames jumped into the river and lifted the casting upon another boat.

Dame Misfortune gave him another kick. He contracted yellow fever in Panama City, thus missing the only boat that stopped at San Diego. With a number of California immigrants also stuck in Panama, he got out the Panama *Herald*, printed half in English, half in Spanish. He finally caught a San Francisco-bound ship, which sprang a leak and nearly sank. His troubles, he said, "would have disheartened any but a 'live Yankee.'"

Finally, he got back to San Diego from San Francisco. As William Heath Davis, the founder of New Town, had lent him nearly $1,000 to set up shop, Ames put out his publication in New Town in 1851. When New Town failed, he removed the *Herald* to Old Town and a second-floor location in a building at the northwest corner of the plaza.

In the *Herald*, Ames championed Senator Gwin's schemes to make San Diego a great city. But he also made enemies. A man with a short temper that had once led him to kill in anger, hardly knowing his own strength, he lost friends through his sharp pen. To those who criticized his policies, he wrote, "I don't give a damn whether you like it or not." And his creditors wondered about his solvency.

The big man in the tall silk hat became a familiar figure around the plaza and in its saloons. Old Towners called him "Boston," as he wrote under that name, or "Judge." In 1852, he became Associate Judge of the Court of Sessions. He boasted of San Diego's future, backing up his prophecy by buying 28 lots.

But he was known better for his frequent absences. Apparently, Senator Gwin wangled a steamer pass for him. He traveled often to San Francisco to mend political fences and arrange for advertising. He liked traveling, even though no coastal steamer had a berth long enough for his Gargantuan body. At bedtime, two tables were shoved together in the salon and stacked with mattresses.

ONE OF GWIN'S SCHEMES appeared near success in 1854. Ames was overjoyed. Wild excitement swept California. Military adventurers seized the mineral-rich peninsula south of San Diego. They proclaimed the Republic of Lower California.

Filibuster William Walker had sailed through the Golden Gate with his tiny private army. Their bark passed San Diego, where the *Herald* blew Walker's trumpet call of American expansionism. They sailed to La Paz. The insurgents kidnapped the Mexican governor. Walker proclaimed himself president under the American flag.

Then came reports of disaster. Trickling back came word of Walker's men starving. The United States refused to take possession. Worse, federal authorities in San Francisco blocked badly needed supplies and reinforcements from leaving the Bay Area. Desperate, Walker marched his troops back to the American border and into the hands of army troops.

Three years later came another promising beginning. At 11 a.m. on August 31, 1857, Ames and an old sea captain began an ear-piercing 100-anvil salute. The first transcontinental mail route had established its western terminus at San Diego. The *Herald* cheered, "Today arrived the first mail from San Antonio, Texas, making the journey in thirty-four traveling days. San Diego is rejoicing."

Old Town, long a prisoner of its geography, had broken out. Following the southern mail route came passenger coach travel. The *Herald* fervently hoped this route would in time become the long-anticipated Southern Pacific transcontinental railway. Two new hotels opened. The big boom was coming.

Alas, San Diego missed the train. Not only was

the Southern Pacific many years away, but the town lost its initial advantage. The "Jackass Mail," as it came to be known, was replaced by the Butterfield stages. Butterfield used a southern route to Warner's Ranch, but by-passed San Diego, turning north to Los Angeles and San Francisco.

The third leg of Gwin's plan also failed: the splitting of California. While geographical division produced heated north-south debates in the state legislature, the legislators couldn't agree to separate. That is, until 1859. Then a bill to create two states did pass both houses. The United States Congress, however, killed it.

Aside from the collapse of Gwin's dreams, Old Town seemed on its last legs. Drought and bad times caused many to pack up and depart. The *Herald* ran column after column of legal notices. Despairing merchants sued hapless rancheros and farmers. Ames's own debts mounted. He could not repay William Heath Davis his loan.

Misfortune dogged Ames. In March 1857, his wife, whom he had married in 1855, died. Not long afterward, unknown parties mutilated her gravestone. In October, a freak gale blew down his home, "Cozy Cottage." Dispirited, broken in health, he gave way to the bottle.

Then rays of sunshine shone. He met a woman that boosted his spirits. He married her and, in November 1859, boasted of a son. The following spring, word spread like lightning of a gold strike near San Bernardino. Gold-seekers came, first in a trickle, then a flood. San Bernardino became a bedlam of excitement.

The town lacked a newspaper. In an increasingly precarious situation in Old Town, "Boston" listened to San Bernardino leaders urging him to move his Washington press north. He did. Closing his office off the plaza, he moved his family and equipment. In

June 1860, he published the first issue of the San Bernardino *Herald*.

But an ill wind nipped at his heels. His paper didn't prosper. His debts overwhelmed him. Ames sold the *Herald*. Now, he had nothing. His golden dreams had turned out to be fool's gold.

On the streets of San Bernardino, "Boston" wandered about, a sad hulk of a man. He went on the drink, seeking oblivion in drunken stupor.

Judge Ames died on July 28, 1861. The doctor scratched on his death certificate, "Apoplexy." But his few Old Town confidants knew better. "Boston" had drunk himself to death. He had not reached his fortieth birthday.

GEORGE DERBY IN LOVE

*Oh my what a trying thing it is for a feller
To git kooped up in this ere little plais
Where the males dont run reglar no how
Nor the females nuther, cos there aint none.*

THUS WAILED THE FORLORN poet laureate of Old Town, George Derby, an Army engineer in town in 1853 and 1854 to dam the San Diego River. In his poem, "Sandyago," Lieutenant Derby lamented that life was mainly an affair of men among men "in this ere little plais."

Still, the Massachusetts-born officer presented the very picture of jollity. His two hundred roly-poly pounds on a medium frame betrayed a fondness for the pleasures of the table. Dark hair and a full beard rounded his cheery face. And Derby possessed twinkling blue eyes that couldn't look on a bald head without an irresistible urge to draw a map of China on it.

Nor was San Diego as womanless as in his doggerel. Occasionally, bachelor Derby climbed on a wagon at midnight with other gay blades from the garrison, intent on serenading young ladies. And there were *bailes* at the *Casa de Bandini*, where he could dance away the night with dark-eyed senoritas in his handsome blue uniform with the gold braid.

There were lonely days, however. The Bandinis would be at their ranch in the back country. Then, he complained to a friend, the place was "dull as though an eclipse had occurred." Besides, he had to contend with small-town gossip. He wrote, "a man can't visit a woman three times consecutively without everybody imagining and saying too (d-m em) that he goes to 'get meat for his cat.'"

Recurrent delays in his project and Old Town's dreariness vexed Derby. In one letter, he grumbled that, if he were stuck "in this tranquil spot" for another six months, the Topographical Engineers would have a vacancy among their second lieutenants. Less obliquely, he later put it in his woebegotten verse:

> *And quick as my business is finished*
> *I shall leave here you may depend on it*
> *By the very first leky steambote,*
> *Or if they are all of em busted*
> *I'll hire a mule from some feller*
> *And just put out to Santy Clara.*

II

"ANY MAN IN THIS COUNTRY," Derby wrote under the pseudonym of John Phoenix, "may marry any woman he pleases—the only difficulty being for him to find any woman that he does please." The jester hadn't found a woman in Old Town that he pleased, at least not for matrimonial purposes. So his hopes soared northward to San Francisco, for he knew far more marriageable lovelies were there.

In late April of 1853, after three months' work on the dam project, he submitted his report to the War Department, complete with surveys and careful drawings. He recommended the river channel be diverted by a dyke into False Bay (Mission Bay), thus preventing the silting of San Diego Bay by the river. His work at a temporary halt, he took a vacation; he boarded the "first leky steambote" to San Francisco.

He established headquarters for himself at the Tehama House, a boarding house, largely billeted by bachelor officers. There he soon earned a certain grudging fame. One day, he surreptitiously changed

68

the menus so that, when the officers came down for dinner that evening, they had a rare selection of gastronomic delicacies, including rat-tail soup, roast mule, and kangaroo cutlet.

Hoaxes were his delight. Another time, while waiting for a carriage trip to begin, he became acquainted with two waiting passengers. He informed each, when he had him alone, that the other was nearly stone-deaf. In the carriage, Derby introduced the two men to each other. Then he sat back with a melancholic, yet sympathetic countenance, while the two men shouted at each other for fifteen minutes.

But one thing excited Derby more than a merry prank: the prospect of romance. He pranced through the Streets of San Francisco with a light heart. Then it happened. One day, mutual friends introduced him to Mary Angeline Coons. She came of a prosperous St. Louis family. Her brother had trekked to California in 1849 and made good; his widowed mother and sister followed. But what captivated Derby was Mary's dark beauty.

Their gay courtship turned to endearment, and endearment turned to love. And love turned to dreams of matrimony. But some of Derby's friends objected. Mary was too old, they said. Never mind that he was six years her senior, she was all of twenty-four— considered in 1853 a hoary age for a bride.

The Coons family joined the objectors—but from Mary's side. How could a penniless second lieutenant support her in the manner she was accustomed to? And with the tales of Derby's flippancy to his superior officers, what future did he have in the Army? So, while he was certainly an amusing fellow, the Coonses thought him a madcap, devoid of any practical sense.

In his defense, Derby could point to a distinguished family tree. Branches featured colony founders, merchant princes, a Governor of Massachusetts, and even a Harvard president. But, alas, his family had fallen on hard times. His father, a lawyer, turned eccentric and deserted his family, ending his days hawking razors on the streets of Boston. Indeed, straitened circumstances made a military career attractive to Derby.

Yet, the humorist could augment his meager salary. His hilarious sketches had been reprinted and reprinted, until all of California roared. His Squibob satires alone made him a celebrity in San Francisco. So he could supplement his income dashing off newspaper and magazine pieces. Besides, in booming California, he could pick up money in off-duty surveying.

All this acrimony produced tension for the pair. In a final twist of their agony, they had a lovers' spat. George lost his composure. He swore to Mary that he would leave San Francisco. And he wouldn't return until the Coons clan had left the city. Indignant, yet crushed, he took a steamer back to San Diego in August.

III

BACK IN OLD TOWN, Derby found a diversion from love's miseries. Judge "Boston" Ames, boss of the local Democrats and publisher of the party organ, the San Diego *Herald*, offered him the job of interim editor. Confident the Democrats already had the upcoming gubernatorial election in the bag, Ames wished to be with the state party bigwigs when the spoils of victory were handed out.

With his usual aplomb, Derby accepted. And in the very next issue, he pulled his great prank. The rock-ribbed Democratic sheet came out for the opposition Whig reform candidate, William Waldo! In the column where previously the Herald had endorsed the Democrat, Governor Bigler, now appeared:

For Governor:
WILLIAM WALDO

The story is that "Boston," unaware of the editorial switch of his paper, was pressing Governor Bigler at the time. Bragging of his political adroitness, he was demanding a larger share of the spoils. Then a barely civil Bigler whipped out a copy of the traitorous *Herald* and shoved it into the face of the dumb-founded Ames!

More distress lay ahead. On election day, Waldo showed surprising strength. He carried San Diego County—thanks to prankster Derby. The Whigs swept San Francisco. Only the Democrtic machine's big majorities in Los Angeles and San Bernardino Counties and in northern California enabled Bigler to squeak through.

Meanwhile, in Old Town, Derby set the town quaking with fear for the terrible revenge which the Gargantuan Ames would inflict on Derby on his return. Derby shuddered in the *Herald* before the extremity of his wrath, [he might] "inflict some grievous bodily injury on me, all of which would be intensely disagreeable." Then, still shaking in his boots, he presented an account—before the fact—of what happened:

> ...a step, a heavy step, was heard upon the stairs, and "Boston" stood before us.... We rose and with an unfaltering voice said, "Well, Judge, how do you do. "He made no reply but commenced taking off his coat.

Derby and the printers prepared to do battle with the mercurial-tempered Ames. Derby removed his coat and cravat. In his account, however, he spares the reader the gore of the first five rounds, settling for a description of the final round:

The sixth, and last, round is
described by the pressman as having been fearfully scientific. We
held "Boston" down over the press
by our nose (which we had insert-
ed between his teeth for that pur-
pose), and while our hair was em-
ployed in holding one of his hands,
we held the other in our left, and
...shouted to him, "Say Waldo."

IV

DERBY COULDN'T GET OVER MARY Coons. He wrote
of the possibilities of matrimony in letters to his
friends. He even had his beloved in mind when he
devised a name puzzle in the *Herald:*

> I am a word of five letters:
> My 1st, and 2nd, is a partner in many a firm;
> My 1st, 2nd, and 3rd, is the note of a bird;
> My 3rd and 4th, is the watchword of victory;
> My 1st, 2nd, 3rd and 4th, is a quadruped;
> My whole is the embodiment of Whig principles
> and the name of an exceedingly lovely lady.

Still, he had his pride and his family honor to
defend. What was he supposed to do, if the Coonses
didn't consider him suitable son-in-law material?
Beg on his knees for Mary's hand? Besides, there was
the matter of his word. He'd sworn irrevocably never
to return to San Francisco until the Coons family
had departed.

Mary waited patiently for her errant lover to
regain his senses. But stubborn George did not,
carrying on a war of nerves into the winter. Mary
also had a rear guard tug-of-war with her family.
Her mother decided to return to St. Louis and wanted
to take Mary with her. Mary tarried, hoping that
George would come for her. It all seemed so hope-
less; in those days, a young lady in her situation
could do little else but sigh, cry, and obey her
mother.

But Mary had pluck. She would defy convention. She set a love trap for George. She knew she would be criticized for such unladylike conduct, but why should she let fear of tongue-waggers deny her her chance for happiness and a family of her own? And why couldn't a woman pull a prank as well as a man?

What if George, she thought, learned that she and her mother had departed San Francisco——but actually had not? Wouldn't he rush to the city in despair, to see if it were indeed true? So one day, a San Francisco newspaper listed Mrs. Coons and her daughter, Mary, as departing by steamer. When George spotted the item in the San Francisco newspaper in San Diego, he grabbed the next sidewheeler north, his heart doubtless palpitating.

There she was! Separated four months, they could only helplessly fall into each other's arms. Love had conquered pride——with a slight assist from Mary. She had out-hoaxed the most famous hoaxster in California.

Magically, all barriers fell away from the newly united couple. In January, 1854, this item appeared in a San Francisco paper:

MARRIED

In Trinity Church, San Francisco,
January 14th, by the Rev. Dr. Clark,
Lieut. George H. Derby, U.S.Corps of
Topographical Engineers, to Mary A.
Coons of St. Louis, Mo.

Immediately after the ceremony,
the bridal party repaired on board
the steamer, **Southerner**, after par-
taking of a magnificent **dejeuner a
la fourchette**, given in honor of
the occurrence by J. Nugent, Esq.,
and other friends, and sailed at 4
p.m. for San Diego.

The newlyweds set up house on Harney Street. Their charming two-story house had been prefabricated in Massachussets and bought by Juan Bandini,

George Derby at the time of his graduation from West Point

before it became their "honeymoon cottage." It had an adobe wing as a kitchen. Mary was delighted. "I have a pretty, little two-story frame house, furnished with much taste—I am proud of my establishment, because it was fitted up by my dear husband. ...I have three beautiful birds—two canaries and a China bird—four pots of flowers.... Our dearest George is below, puffing away at his pipe as usual."

George could puff away contentedly. "It is impossible for anyone to be happier in the married state of life than I have been and still am," he

74

wrote. "My wife is everything that could be desired, gentle, amiable, and nice. She is far from being extravagant and is in fact the best 'poor man's wife' that could be found..."

Derby was happy in Old Town. He had completed the dyke in the river and now awaited a further appropriation to construct the protecting levee. Consequently, he had little military duty, affording him time for odd surveying jobs and dashing off funny sketches. This extra money allowed him to hire an elderly manservant, who usually got drunk on the Sabbath.

Derby thoroughly enjoyed domestic life. He pleased his palate with Mary's cooking. He smoked his pipe contentedly. Or he got in his wife's way. She, he noted, "has come out very strong in the culinary line....I pass my time mostly in hugging her (& getting all over flour)...."

*The tale of a thief who would
not let Old Town forget him.*

THE GHOST OF
YANKEE JIM

IN THE BITTER WINTER of 1849, Ben Currier heard an intriguing rumor at Barnes Gap on the North Fork of the American River. A mysterious character named Yankee Jim had made a rich strike and was bringing in big nuggets in his pouch to the trading camp. Gold-seeker Currier and five of his cronies, yearning to get in on the strike, decided to follow Yankee Jim to his secret camp.

One night, the six trailed the big, burly miner out of town, but Yankee Jim gave them the slip. The disappointed party moved in with two other miners in a canyon to look by day for the yellow outcroppings and keep an eye open for Yankee Jim.

Currier, out on his own one day, followed a ridge in Busby Canyon. He came upon a man sleeping under a bark shelter. Surprised, the man on the ground explained that he was worried about protection, as he had run out of bullets for his gun. Currier promised to get him some bullets. Grateful, the miner said if Currier kept the location of the strike a secret, he'd make it worth his while.

Ben Currier returned to his camp. He got some spare bullets and returned to Busby Canyon without telling his companions what had happened. In appreciation, the miner told Currier about his find and offered to share it with Currier. They got to talking, and the man admitted to being Yankee Jim. He claimed to be a native of Maine. Before the gold rush, he said, he jumped ship and "combed the beach" along the California coast.

The secret of the strike, however, was too big

76

for Currier. Probably feeling obligated to his five friends, he told them the location. Word spread like wildfire from the five until a thousand miners were scratching the earth in Busby Canyon.

A disgusted Yankee Jim moved on.

Whether the loss of a possible fortune soured Yankee Jim on the human race is unknown. What is known is that he turned to a rather revengeful occupation—stealing other people's horses. It was certainly lucrative and far less strenuous than digging. Indeed, he became so adept at it that he had to build a log corral for all his stolen horses.

He made good money at it, too. Any transportation

in the Mother Lode brought top dollar. Horses, which normally sold for $6, would bring up to $300 at the diggings, all saddled and ready to ride. Of course, living expenses strained credulity, too. A slice of bread cost a dollar, and it cost another dollar to butter it.

Entrepreneur Yankee Jim thrived. That is, until the level of lawlessness reached such proportions that the miners demanded retribution. After a rogues' gallery of cutthroats descended on the gold country, miners' committees formed to issue summary justice.

The penchant of these committees to hand out "hemp cravats" caused Yankee Jim to pause. After woeful consideration of the odds on his longevity if he remained in the hills, he saddled his best horse and cut stick for the coast.

He stopped in Stockton. There, with two others, he took up his trade again. The trio filched and sold horses, working their way southward toward hell-whooping Los Angeles. Beyond that lay San Diego, which, while known as a law-and-order burgh, offered desperados the advantage of close proximity to the Mexican border.

II

ON THE EVENING of Friday, August 13, 1852, Captain James Keating happened to be standing on a pier at La Playa on Point Loma. He noticed a man in a red shirt take a rowboat from the beach and row toward Keating's untended schooner, the *Plutus*. Disturbed, Keating called out:

"Whose boat is that?"

The man shouted back that it was his own. Knowing this to be false, the captain demanded the man return the dingy to shore or else be fired upon. The man in the rowboat muttered something unintelligible to Keating and continued to row out into the channel.

Raising his shotgun to his shoulder, Keating aimed at the red shirt and pulled the trigger. The buckshot fell short, dropping harmlessly into the water. The man in the rowboat changed course, now rowing toward the ocean, parallel to the shore. Some distance from Keating, he rowed to shore, ditched the rowboat, and escaped through the bushes up the hill.

The following morning, the captain reported the incident to the authorities in Old Town. Mayor Tebbett, Judge Hays, Deputy Sheriff Reiner, and Sheriff Crosthwaite set out to find the man in the red shirt. While searching False Bay (Mission Bay), they turned up and caught two suspicious-looking men, but not the man in the red shirt.

Later, Deputy Sheriff Reiner rode out to continue the search. He stopped to tell the Mexican caretaker at Rose's Ranch north of Old Town to be on the lookout. If he should see the fellow in the red shirt, he should make every effort to apprehend him.

That evening, a man in a red shirt did appear at the door of the caretaker, asking for food. After eating, the man lay down to rest, but became suspicious of the movements of the Mexican. He made for the door and began running. The caretaker's wife quickly handed her husband a lasso and an old artillery sword.

He gave chase. After a hundred yards, he began to gain on the man. The caretaker whirled his rope over his head and threw it over the escapee's head, pinning his arms to his side. The man struggled to free himself. A tremendous whack on the head with the rusty old sword brought him to the ground with a ghastly wound over the ear. The caretaker lashed the man to a mule and led him into Old Town by midnight.

The next morning, the committee of citizens interrogated the three captives. The man in the red shirt was James Robinson, known as Yankee Jim. His two confederates were William Harris and James Grayson Loring. As the San Diego *Herald* put it, "before night [they] persuaded them that they had better own up." The trio confessed to having come down from Stockton, stealing and selling horses. In Old Town, they had sold their horses and bought provisions, then attempted to steal the *Plutus* to make their way to Lower California.

The arrests and confessions created a whirl of excitement in Old Town. The town had suffered from a crime wave for the last year and a half. It started with San Francisco volunteers who came to town to help suppress the Garra Uprising, even though the Indian revolt never fully materialized. They satisfied their yearning for a fight by roaring through the town on drunken sprees.

The sheriff and the courts were unable to curb the lawlessness. A Mexican girl was raped. A man lost his life and his money belt when he took a dip in the San Diego River. Horses were stolen. The mood of the town can be assessed from a brief item in the *Herald* of July 10, 1851:

HORSE THIEVES

Mayor Tebbetts had his horse stolen on Wed. night about 12:00 from his very door. If thieves are caught they will be hung up to the flagstaff in the Plaza without trial.

The mood turned sullen in the summer of 1852. Persistent hot winds blew from the desert, aggravating the general irritability. The water supply was limited. Drought threatened pastures for livestock and crops in the backcountry. Yankee Jim couldn't

have picked a worse time or place to run afoul of
the law.

The three prisoners were bound over to the Court
of Sessions. The grand jury brought in a charge of
grand larceny against Yankee Jim and William Harris
and charged James Grayson Loring with being an accessory before the fact. Harris and Loring were arraigned separately, found guilty, and sentenced to
one year in the state prison each.

The trial of Yankee Jim opened on August 17,
1852, at the <u>Plaza Court House</u>, just three days
after he received the severe head wound at Rose's
Ranch. Judge John Hays presided. Yankee Jim served
as his own attorney and exercised his right to
challenge four of the prospective jurymen. At about
two o'clock, the jury retired to deliberate. Some
thirty minutes later, the jury returned. The foreman
submitted the verdict:

> Your jurors in the within case of James Robin-
> son [Yankee Jim's real name] have the honor to
> return a verdict of guilty and do therefore sen-
> tence him to be hanged by the neck until dead.

September 18 was hanging day. Yankee Jim was put
on a wagon on the grounds of what is now the Whaley
House on San Diego Avenue. A scaffold had been
erected from two beams and an iron crossbar. Yankee
Jim talked with Sheriff Crosthwaite, still disbe-
lieving he would hang, perhaps thinking this was a
hoax to scare him half to death as punishment.

He was ordered to stand. Crosthwaite adjusted the
noose around his neck. Asked if he had any final
words to say, Yankee Jim harangued the crowd at
length. Finally, the sheriff gave orders to whip the
mules and pull the wagon from beneath him, removing
the last doubt and hope of Yankee Jim.

The hanging, however, didn't go exactly according
to plan. The scaffolding hadn't been erected high
enough, considering that Yankee Jim was six feet,

three or four inches tall. The fall didn't break his neck. Instead, he slowly strangled to death. The following morning, the doctor pronounced him dead, and Crosthwaite cut him down.

III

IN THE SUMMER of 1966, thirty players reenacted the trial and hanging of Yankee Jim at the Whaley House and yard. During the rehearsals and perform-ances of the play, Frances Bardacke's *The Ballad of Yankee Jim*, the cast spent considerable time in the Whaley House, dressed in their gingham dresses and frock coats.

Several players reported strange happenings. The most common were odd upstairs noises—the sound of a heavy man with boots walking upstairs. On investiga-tion, they saw nobody. Once, a cast member looked up the stairway and saw a man standing on the landing. The actor walked up the stairs, walked clear through the man, took a step into the room, and turned to face the man, who almost immediately faded and disappeared.

These and other odd occurrences make good ghost yarns, to be added to tales of the other resident spooks of the Whaley House museum. They may be explained away as the product of lively imaginations of cast members, especially in the emotionally charged situation of reenacting a trial and nasty execution.

What is harder to explain away, however, is that Yankee Jim haunts the conscience of those familiar with his case. The man who got hung for stealing a rowboat will not let Old Town forget the question of whether the punishment fit the crime. Perhaps a modern re-trial, if only a mock one, might ease the citizenry's conscience and let Yankee Jim, at last, rest in peace.

82

THE ORDEAL OF
MARY   WALKER

ON THE MORNING OF JULY 5, 1865, a sidewheeler looped around the lofty cape of Point Loma. From a stateroom stepped a petite schoolmarm from Massachusetts. Mary Chase Walker by name, she had a comely face and figure and wore her long, dark hair in curls. But her complexion was wan and pale, and she viewed *terra firma* with vast relief.

The three-day voyage had been debilitating for this New England spinster. She suffered from seasickness. Miss Walker wondered if she could face her first class the next morning. Fortunately for her, a black stewardess aboard the steamer sympathized with her plight and eased her discomfort.

From shipboard, she stared at the sunblasted landscape. Born and raised in the lush greenery of New England, she was disheartened by the unfamiliar surroundings. "The hills were brown and barren," she recalled, "not a tree or green thing to be seen."

As the sidewheeler churned the waters of the inner bay, Miss Walker spotted several houses and a military barrack on land. This couldn't be the town, she thought. Incredulous, she asked the captain, "Is this San Diego?"

With a mischievous twinkle in his eyes, he replied, "No, the town is four miles away." The twinkle she interpreted to mean, "Won't the Yankee school ma'am be surprised when she sees the town."

She was. Crude, vermin-infested, mud huts surrounded a dirt square. The primitive sanitation, combined with animal droppings in the streets, mixed

with the smell of chili and enchiladas, assaulted
her nostrils. "Of all the dilapidated, miserable-
looking places I have ever seen," she thought, "this
was the worst."

Miss Walker was far from neat clapboard build-
ings, verdant commons, and dignified New Englanders.
The Americans here were an enclave of coarse Southern and Northern "copperheads," who had sympathized
with the South in the recent Civil War. Their prin-
cipal amusement seemed to be hard-drinking — followed by cussing, tobacco-spitting, and shooting at
each other. No place for a lady.

Her maidenly sensibilities were in for more
shocks. Driven by wagon to a tavern on San Diego
Avenue, the Colorado House, she found she was the
only woman in the establishment. The uneasy inn-
keeper offered her the use of the kitchen. Looking
into the kitchen, she observed the Indian cook, sit-
ting on a bench in front of an open sack of flour,
vigorously scratching his head.

She didn't sleep well that first night — she had
bed companions. "The fleas were plentiful and hungry," she remembered. Mary Walker also got a bucolic,
unofficial welcome to the town: a weird sound sent
her to her window where she discovered a donkey
below, saluting her with an unearthly bray.

She bemoaned her fate. Now she understood why
sixty unemployed teachers in San Francisco—all
ahead of her on the waiting list for a teaching job
opening—had turned down San Diego. They knew the
town. If only her savings weren't about to run out,
she wouldn't have had to take the position in this
Godforsaken outpost.

Mary Walker's first impulse was to flee. Yet
teaching had been the dream of her childhood. And
hadn't she come to California of her own free will?
Indeed, when New Hampshire slashed her teaching
salary of $400 a year in half during the Civil War,

she thought burgeoning California would do better by its teachers.

That wasn't the only reason. In New England, in her mid-thirties, the chances of marriage were slim. Society considered even the mid-twenties ancient for a bride. But American women were in short supply in the Golden State. Many eligible New England men had struck out for El Dorado. She decided to follow.

So here she was. In California, with a teaching job—at a salary of $65 a month. True, the town was crude and dreary. Yet she was made of stern stuff. With the pluck and perseverance of her Puritan forebears, she would see it through. Mary Walker set her jaws.

II

THE FOLLOWING MORNING, Mary faced her class. She stood in the newly completed one-room schoolhouse. It had a small rear room, with indoor plumbing consisting of a water bucket and a dipper for drinking. Known as the Mason Street School, this green-painted building was the first public school in the county, and Mary Walker was its first instructor.

Her pupils came in different sizes and hues. They ranged in age from about four to seventeen. Some were Americans; a few were English, but most were, as she recalled, "Spanish or half-breed children ....Many American soldiers and some sailors had come to San Diego in the early days and married pretty senoritas,"

She counted forty heads. With such a range of ages—and with only one room—she wondered how she could separate them into grades. She did not try. She adopted the simplest of curricula. "I aimed to teach what would be most meaningful to them, namely, spelling, arithmetic, and how to write letters."

Mary Walker and the Mason Street School

Miss Walker soon encountered irregularity in attendance. Fiesta preparations kept girls out of class. And the boys found lame excuses. "For a week before a bullfight," she explained, "the boys were more or less absent, watching preparations, such as fencing up the streets leading to the plaza."

Tardiness annoyed her, too. The children's parents had a lackadaisical attitude toward time. In her neat Spencerian hand, she penned on her Teacher's Report that tardiness was the rule rather than the exception. "Clocks," she wrote cryptically, "not generally used by the heads of families for marking time..."

However, she made headway. Despite the absenteeism and tardiness, she taught her charges their letters and numbers. Moreover, Mary's employers—the three School Trustees—were pleased with her. Especially appreciative was the President of the School Board, Ephraim W. Morse.

This bearded Old Town merchant and stellar citi-

zen hailed from Mary's home state, Massachusetts.
He understood her problems at the Mason Street
School, too, having once taught school himself. A
kindly, unassuming widower with laughing eyes, Morse
went out of his way to help her adjust to her
strange surroundings.

Mary and Ephraim became fast friends. She learned
he was about the only temperance man in town. Indeed, repentant drunkards sometimes came to his
store for a sermon on the evil of demon rum. An
exemplary Christian, he tried to get the other
merchants to close on the Sabbath, with the result,
however, that only his *tienda* remained shut on
Sundays.

Mary's initial shock wore away. She rented two
unfurnished rooms on the second floor of a house
facing the plaza. As no store sold furniture or
stoves, kind townfolks lent her the necessary pieces
to furnish her rooms. So she took up her own house-
keeping.

And Spanish hospitality charmed her. Native Cali-
fornians seized on any excuse for fiestas that
sometimes lasted for days. With fancy dress parties,
smiling faces and courtly manners, music and endless
dancing, Old Town began to please Mary.

The perky New England schoolmarm could waltz away
the night at *bailes* at the *Casa de Estudillo*.
She dined at elaborate garden dinners, where she
developed a taste for native cuisine. However, she
found that even a small quantity of one sauce—half
and half tomato and chili pepper—"would bring tears
to the most stony eyes."

With the winter rains, the wild flowers came out
and the mountains wore a carpet of green. With the
lovely backcountry, the beautiful bay, and her new
friends, Mary Walker began to feel she had found her
second home.

AFTER NEARLY ELEVEN MONTHS in Old Town, a storm broke over Mary's head. One day, toward the end of May, 1866, she happened to be walking on Juan Street about noontime. Passing Joe Mannasse's *tienda*, she noticed a black woman munching on crackers and cheese. Mary recognized her as the kind stewardess who had helped her when she became seasick on the steamer that brought her to San Diego.

She walked into the store to greet the woman, a light-complected person, a one-fourth Negro, known as a quadroon. With a friendly interest in the stewardess, Mary invited her to a regular lunch with her at the Franklin House. The stewardess accepted. And both of them walked to the tavern.

Then it happened. As the pair entered the dining room and sat down, Mary saw angry stares in her direction. The other patrons arose and indignantly left the restaurant. Mary and her friend had the dining room to themselves.

Word spread. The town talked about nothing else. How the tongues did wag! "You see, we are a high-toned people down here," explained the San Diego correspondent to the readers of the San Francisco *Bulletin,* in the July 14, 1866, issue, "and don't intend to tolerate anything of this kind."

They didn't. The mentor of the school's youth had associated with a black person. Infuriated parents withdrew their children from Mary's school. The enrollment dropped from twenty-six to fifteen. They let it be known that the boycott would end only with the teacher's replacement.

"Now what do you imagine caused the parents to take their children from school?" asked the San Diego correspondent in the *Bulletin*. He laid the scandal to Miss Walker inviting "a lady to dine with

her and visit her school—a lady of respectability
and of education, but who had unfortunately a bit of
Negro blood in her veins."

The plucky teacher vigorously defended herself.
Didn't she have the right to associate with whomever
she pleased? And as far as this being a color issue,
she made the ironic point that the stewardess had a
fairer complexion than some of her accusers.

Still, upset parents demanded the School Trustees
take action against Miss Walker. Complaints were
lodged with Ephraim Morse. The School Trustees met
to decide whether or not to fire Mary.

Trustee David B. Hoffman, a physician with a full
black beard, argued to dismiss her. It wasn't a
question of the merit of the case, he argued. Or her
competency. He agreed to her being a good teacher.
She must be let go, he maintained, in order to keep
the school open.

The state paid Miss Walker's salary. And if enrollment dropped below a certain number, funds would
be cut off. Thus, the boycott would force the school
to close. Dr. Hoffman insisted she be replaced with
another teacher acceptable to the parents.

This angered Trustee Robert D. Israel. The wiz-
ened veteran of the Mexican War stood up for Mary's
right of free association. As to the funds from
Sacramento, he declared defiantly, "I'll be damned
if I wouldn't take the school money and throw it in
the bay as far as I could send it, before I would
dismiss the teacher to please these copperheads."

Dr. Hoffman and Captain Israel debated the issue.
Their heated argument escalated to near blows. Finally, Israel turned to the other Trustee, Ephraim
Morse, and hotly concluded, "You may do as you
please, but I will never consent to her dismissal."

This left the decision to Morse. His opinion,
based on his conviction, as well as his heart, would
be to retain her. An emancipationist, he could not

allow her to be dismissed for merely associating with a black woman. Besides, he had grown fond of the spunky schoolmarm.

It wasn't that simple, however. Mary knew of Ephraim's precarious financial condition. He owed an enormous debt to his wholesaler in San Francisco. A vote to retain her might result in a retaliatory boycott of his store, which meant bankruptcy. He stood to lose everything he had worked so hard for over the years.

And Morse would probably have to leave town. He didn't want to. He came to San Diego for his health and found its therapeutic climate helpful. Besides, he had a vision of a city. It would rise four miles to the south, and he wanted to have a part in its building.

Mary and Ephraim made a difficult decision, one that went against the grain of their moral convictions. Yet, in the circumstances, they considered it the prudent one. Mary resigned her position. The School Trustees hired another teacher, and the crisis ended.

Surprisingly, Mary found another instructing job in San Diego. She tutored a girl in Spring Valley and boarded with the family. There she had a steady gentleman caller—Ephraim Morse. He rode out from Old Town to be with her on Saturday evenings and often stayed over into Sunday.

Mary and Ephraim had much in common. They both had similar New England religious upbringings. They shared liberal views and lively senses of humor. And they had grown together in the school crisis. He proposed to her, and she accepted him. They were married on December 20, 1866.

They were together nearly thirty-three years in married life. In 1868, they moved to the new town started to the south of Old Town. Morse and Alonzo Horton were the co-founders of this new town, which is downtown San Diego today. Ephraim became its best-loved citizen, a leader in every move for its advancement.

Mary took a quieter role. Nothing appealed to her Christian sympathy so much as human suffering. Unostentatiously, she aided the needy. Even her best friends were unaware of her many charitable deeds. But her name was held dear in the humble homes of the poor.

No children were born to their union. However, in a broader sense, they had many children. Ephraim, by being the first to propose the setting aside of a large tract of land for a park, is the Father of Balboa Park, which has delighted generations of young people. And many children will remember the name of Mary Chase Walker. A grateful city memorialized her by naming a school after her: the Mary Chase Walker Elementary School.

THE CALLING OF
HELEN HUNT JACKSON

IN 1879, HELEN HUNT JACKSON felt listless and lonely. Although she was an established writer and poet, she didn't have the heart to put pencil to paper. Her publisher wasn't interested in her latest novel, although she had published nearly three dozen and had a wide following for her romances. She sighed and put the manuscript aside.

There was little romance in her life. At forty-four, she had married a tall Quaker with a Smith Brothers beard, William S. Jackson, a railroad executive. After four years of matrimony, however, they had drifted apart, with little to say to each other or do together. With irony, she wrote her lifetime friend, the poet Emily Dickinson, about 'the man I live with'—"he is in New York— and I live alone..."

It wasn't her first bout with loneliness. At twenty-two, she had married a handsome army officer, Lieutenant Edward B. Hunt, a promising physicist and inventor. Leading the wandering life of an army wife, Mrs. Hunt also endured long spells of separation from her spouse. But she bore him two sons and continued to hope for a duty where the entire family could be together.

A series of numbing tragedies, however, destroyed her family. She lost her nine-month-old son in 1854 to "dropsy on the brain." In 1863, with the Civil War coming to an end, her husband, while working on his invention of a submarine at the Brooklyn Naval

Yard, was killed in a test of the under-water machine. Two years later, diphtheria claimed her dear, precocious, nine-year-old son, Rennie.

She couldn't cry. The cumulative blows were too stunning. The nights were unbearable. She retired into seclusion, except for relatives. In time, she found surcease from her sorrows in poetry. "Oh, iron-handed grief, which holds my soul in searing grief..." she wrote. Besides mourning, she felt useless. Now husbandless and childless, she wrote a friend, "I alone am left, who avail nothing."

Yet, she was of avail. Solace came in verse. Her touching outcry struck a sensitive chord in a nation lamenting the loss of fathers and sons in the internecine War Between the States. An editor accepted her poetry, and she became known by her initials, "H.H." She began to think of writing as a livelihood.

When she was thirty-five, Colonel Thomas Wentworth Higginson, arbiter of American letters and the discoverer of Emily Dickinson, became her mentor. With his encouragement and aid, she became in time one of the most highly paid writers in the nation. She published dozens of short stories, travel sketches, and poems, as well as dozens of popular novels under the pseudonym of Saxe Holm.

But now, in the spring of 1879, she had no heart to write. She was forty-eight. For this plumpish woman, who parted her short blonde hair down the middle, with curls on both sides of her face, life had lost its vital spark. Her life seemed over.

Besides, she lived in a certain isolation. Her husband had bought a home for them in Colorado Springs, Colorado, thousands of miles from her native state of Massachusetts. She missed her relatives and the laughter and bright chatter of her literary cohorts in the East.

Just when her spirits reached low ebb, an old friend invited her to her summer home in Maine. She flew to pack her bags. She would again see the leaves turning yellow and gold. She would visit her friends and talk with her publisher in Boston.

Toward the end of her trip, something happened. She attended a tea party in Boston, a reception for the Omaha Indian Committee. There, she heard Chief Standing Bear and Princess Bright Eyes tell about the Poncas tribe of Nebraska. She heard of their eviction by the government and their forced trek of a thousand miles to barren and untillable land, with great suffering and deaths on their terrible journey.

She was outraged. Her reaction surprised herself, for she was no woman for causes. Neither slavery, women's suffrage, nor Demon Rum had activated her pen. Now, her zealous indignation knew no bounds. "I have become," she wrote a friend, "what I have said a thousand times was the most odious thing in life, 'a woman with a hobby.'"

Helen Hunt Jackson became a crusader. She lectured; she wrote tracts; she circulated petitions; she inundated editors with letters and articles. She denounced the Secretary of the Interior for his indifference to the plight of the Indians. Her devotion to her cause only widened the breach with her husband, who tried to deflect her with stories of Indian atrocities in Colorado.

No matter. She couldn't help herself. She closeted herself in the Astor Library in New York City to research the history of the Great White Father's dealings with the Indians. She found a record of pernicious double-dealing and broken treaties. Mrs. Jackson compiled the facts and figures into a book, *A Century of Dishonor*, published in 1881.

A storm broke over her head. A public led to believe that Indians were "brutal savages" was incredulous. Letters poured in, disputing her accounts and conclusions. Reviewers called her book hysterical and unbelievable.

Mrs. Jackson was equally unrelenting. At her own expense, she had her publisher, Harper Brothers, send a copy of her book to each member of Congress, with a quotation from Benjamin Franklin printed in red on the cover: "Look upon your hands! They are stained with the blood of your relations." Then she followed up with lobbying visits to each Congressman and Senator.

A conscience-stricken minority rallied to the

cause, recognizing the need to redeem what she called this "stain of dishonor." The influential Indian Rights Association was founded. Congress passed a bill compensating the Poncas and letting them choose their land. A Presidential Commission returned a report favorable to the Indians. The tide began to turn.

II

IN MARCH, 1882, THE SIDE-WHEELER, *S. S. Orizaba*, wheezed into the quiet harbor of San Diego. A poised lady writer looked from the deck at the small houses on the hills. Helen Hunt Jackson had come to research four articles for *Century Magazine* on the Missions and Mission Indians.

Her California junket had been planned with her husband, Will. On the day of her departure from New York, however, he telegraphed her that he couldn't come. Helen was furious. She wrote a friend that she was "too mad to unpack and too restless to work—generally demoralized." She went alone.

She came to San Diego with letters of introduction, one to the selfless Ephraim Morse. Mrs. Jackson felt immediately at ease with Morse and his wife, Mary Chase Morse, all three hailing from Massachusetts. Morse helped her in finding material on local Indians.

She saw Indians. She attended trials involving Indian offenders. She saw crude, nondescript hovels on hills and in canyons, where pathetic, dispossessed Dieguenos survived. "Most of these Indians are miserable," she wrote in her article; "worthless beggars, drunkards, of course, and worse."

Another contact let her meet Indians. Father Anthony Ubach, who came to San Diego in 1866, lived in the abandoned Casa de Estudillo in Old Town and visited the Indian villages. He baptized the children, married the youths, ministered to the sick and bereaved, and saw to it that the people had sufficient food and medical care.

Between puffs of his ever-present cigar, the beloved Father Ubach related many tales to Mrs. Jackson about the redskins and the white man. One, in particular, stuck in her mind. It concerned two runaway lovers. He related how a young Indian and a maiden came to his adobe chapel on Conde Street one night to be married.

In a two-horse, double-seat carriage, Mrs. Jackson and Father Ubach visited the decaying missions and the old ranchos, such as the elegant adobe hacienda of Rancho Guajome with its twenty rooms. With such glimpses of a romantic never-never land, she perceived a pastoral Arcady, peopled by gentle Franciscan priests, generous rancheros, and simple, but noble Indians.

In contrast, she saw the miserable plight of the Mission Indians. Everywhere it was the same bitter tale of eviction from ancestral lands. In Temecula, for example, the sheriff arrived in 1875 with a posse to move the Indians from some twenty-two hundred acres of rich farming land along the Temecula River. The posse moved them only three miles, yet their new location was another world. Mrs. Jackson found Pechanga Canyon to be a humid, barren canyon with rocky buttes on both sides and without a stream of water. "Every face, except those of the very young," she wrote, "was sad beyond description."

In beautiful San Pasqual Valley, she found only one dirty, ragged, and nearly blind Indian. And this on land set apart by President Grant in 1870 as the San Pasqual Reservation. But the Great White Father had revoked the order the following year.

Everywhere, she saw the sad faces of the Indians. On her trip north, she visited Indians about to be evicted from their land thirty-five miles from San Bernardino. She saw a baby lying ill in a cradle of twigs woven together. The child's mother silently prayed over her.

When Mrs. Jackson asked about a doctor for the baby, the mother replied with quivering lips, "We sent for a doctor to come to the village to see if he could cure my little one, but he refused to come. He told my husband ... to bring her to San Bernardino, but she is too ill to bear the journey."

Mrs. Jackson protested what she had seen. She bombarded the Department of Indian Affairs with letters. In her outcry of moral indignation, she pointed to America's black record of Indian treatment. She pleaded that if the small remnant of Mission Indians were to be saved, it must be done speedily.

In July, she got her chance. She was appointed Special Commissioner of Indian Affairs in Southern California to investigate Indian conditions and to see whether suitable land could be made available to them. After research, she co-authored a report, *Conditions and Needs of the Mission Indians.*

The report, however, gathered dust from the beginning in a Washington office. Congress did not act. She realized that the government got away with its shifty Indian policy because of public hatred for the Indians, or indifference to their problems. Something must be done to alter dramatically the public conception of Indians. She must touch the conscience of the nation.

III

"IT WAS SHEEP-SHEARING TIME in Southern California," Helen wrote rapidly with a pencil on a long, yellow sheet. She scribbled at what she described to Higginson as "lightning speed." She turned out two to three thousand finished words a day. "I have never done <u>half</u> the amount of work in the same time." She felt that an outside power drove her.

Mrs. Jackson began on December 1, 1883. She wrote the opening line in a rented room at the Berkeley Hotel on Fifth Avenue in New York City. While far from the novel's locale, she decorated the room with the rich colors of Indian memorabilia. When she paused, she could look out of her window at the heavy snow falling on Fifth Avenue.

She had the novel set in her mind. It had come to her in a flash. The scene would be Southern California; the time, when Mission bells rang. On her desk stood a photograph of the head of a young man and a beautiful maiden, in a halo of clouds. They would be her hero and heroine: he an Indian sheepshearer named Alessandro, she a half-breed named Ramona.

In the severe winter, Mrs. Jackson developed a sore throat. She didn't feel well. After writing in furious spurts, she collapsed on her bed, utterly spent. All through the winter, she alternated between writing bouts and exhaustion. She didn't know whether to blame the frantic pace or the miserable weather.

She did know she couldn't stop. As if by compulsion, she wrote as if she must write now or never. "Twice, since beginning it I have broken down for a week," she wrote Higginson. "What I have to endure in holding myself away from it, no words can tell. It is like keeping from a lover, whose hands I can reach."

Before April, she completed the twenty-sixth and last chapter. Incredibly, Helen Hunt Jackson had written 150,000 words in four months. *Ramona* was done.

She had wild hopes for the novel. Congress and the people had largely ignored her *A Century of Dishonor*; she now offered the same, bitter message, but as a love story. "I have sugared the pill," she wrote. She hoped *Ramona* would do for the Indian what *Uncle Tom's Cabin* did for the blacks.

Spring came. But her health did not improve. Finally, in mid-May, she called a doctor about her mysterious ailment that was debilitating her. The doctor apparently didn't know what was wrong with her, either, as he advised her to refrain from "brain work" and to stay away from the cold Colorado climate. But, willful as ever, she took the train for Colorado Springs.

Then *Ramona* came out. Her friends were enthusiastic, and when it first appeared in serial form in a magazine, it won instant success. Then the reviews came in. The New York *Times* labeled it a "romance." Critics called it a tender love story, set in a pastoral Arcady of Franciscan padres and Spanish Dons.

Helen was stunned. Critics read her book simply as a historical romance of a vanished time. After reading the review in *The Atlantic Monthly*, she wrote an old friend, "Not one word for my Indians! I put my heart and soul in the book for them. It is a dead failure."

Her health continued to deteriorate. Unable to keep food on her stomach, she lost forty pounds. Her face became yellow and wan. She feared she had malaria. Learning of a homeopathic physician in San Francisco, she moved there. Hoping that his pills could bring her back to health, she was overjoyed by a slight improvement in her condition.

She wrote her husband and wondered why he didn't visit her. She found out. She had talked to a young writer, unaware that her remarks would be published in a magazine article. Mr. Jackson accused Helen of

100

talking too freely to this newspaper woman. He was chagrined by her views on several well-known writers and also, she felt, because she had mentioned him as well.

In early April, she suffered a relapse. She could sit up only long enough to have her bed made up. Realizing she would be bedridden for some time, she found a room on Russian Hill with a magnificient view of San Francisco Bay. Remembering the pleasure of her trips to Yosemite, she wondered if the pure air of the forest might cure her.

She wrote to John Muir, asking him to be her guide to the Sierras. She wrote "that nothing except three months out of doors day and night will get the poison out of my veins." He kindly replied, urging her to go to the mountains. "The pines will spread their healing arms about you and bless you and make you well again."

But she wouldn't get well. By the end of July, she knew she would never see Vernal Falls again. She was dying of cancer. She wrote her final words to Colonel Higginson. "My 'Century of Dishonor' and 'Ramona' are the only things I have done for which I am glad now. The rest is of no moment. They will live on and they will bear fruit. They already have."

She wrote her final letter on August 8, 1885, addressed to President Grover Cleveland. "I ask you to read my 'Century of Dishonor.' I am dying happier in the belief I have that it is your hand that is destined to strike the first steady blow towards lifting the burden of infamy from our country..."

Four days later, John Muir rang her doorbell. Nobody answered the door. The shades were drawn. When he returned to his home, he told his wife, "Mrs. Jackson may have gone somewhere." She had. Within the hour of his ringing her doorbell, she had died.

Emily Dickinson wrote Mr. Jackson. "Helen of Troy

will die, but Helen of Colorado, never. 'Dear friend, can you walk?' were the last words I wrote her— 'Dear friend, I can fly'— her immortal reply."

will die, but Helen of Colorado, never. 'Dear friend, can you walk?' were the last words I wrote her— 'Dear friend, I can fly'— her immortal reply."

THE DUTCH COURAGE
OF JOSHUA SLOANE

A SPRY LITTLE ANTIC named Joshua Sloane appeared on the sand-strewn streets of Old Town in the early 1850s. This small Irishman had an open face, light brown hair, and sideburns that ended in chin whiskers. He had one wall eye, the other a sparkling blue one, which, when not alert for bypassing, pretty senoritas, gingerly guided its owner around horse-droppings.

Sloane became known for his unusual creativity. One day, for instance, he looked up at Presidio Hill, and an idea popped into his head. He had workmen erect a windmill with six sails, each twenty feet long, at the crest of the hill. The turning sails powered stones that ground wheat. His mill produced eight barrels of flour daily.

Sometimes, he used his lively imagination to pull people's legs. In 1872, a newspaper reported he was promoting $20,000 for a pioneer venture in a novel energy source. He asked, Why not harness the power of the denizen of the Pacific—whales?

Sloane proposed to propel ships by whale power. The migratory pattern of whales, he pointed out, paralleled the Pacific coast shipping lanes. Doubtless with a straight face, he told of encouraging experiments he had conducted in False Bay (Mission Bay) with two young whales.

Another inspiration cost him his job. In 1856, when he taught at the school house on the plaza, a little varmint succeeded in exhausting Josh's patience. Struck with an idea, the schoolmaster removed one of his shoes, grabbed the miscreant, and held his nose to the fetid stocking. The school trustees, however, took a dim view of this punishment. They ended his pedagogic career.

He also earned a reputation as an eccentric. Few knew him well. If left alone, a certain serenity suffused his face, as if his mind were in another time and place. He was a shy man. He lived out his allotted years in boarding houses, preferring the company of his dog or cat to human society. He once informed a reporter he was teaching his cat to play the Jew's harp.

Paradoxically, Sloane wasn't meek in matters of principle. In a town full of Democrats, he stood virtually alone as a Republican. He spoke out boldly and fearlessly against the institution of slavery. He campaigned for the election of the Illinois railsplitter, Abe Lincoln. And Sloane organized the Republican Party in San Diego.

Sloane was an enigma. Ordinarily a sensitive and retiring soul, he could be the bravest man in town. Without fear, he proclaimed views that might bring him a sound thrashing. Shy, yet he ogled every pretty, young woman. He dressed as a Beau Brummel and acted, when the mood struck him, the part of a gallant. Yet, when asked as an older gentleman why he didn't court the mature ladies of the town, he snapped, "Rather kiss a rat-trap than an old woman."

The answer lay in his drinking. Nearly everyone in Old Town tippled, of course. They guzzled for different reasons. Some for sociability, others to drown their homesickness and loneliness. Sloane found something else in the bottle—Dutch courage. The invigorating fluid released him from his timidity. It emboldened him. Under the influence, his voice and pen waxed eloquent.

This strange mixture of strong convictions and ardent spirits turned him into the town's consummate politician. Not the back-slapping politico, but a canny Irishman capable of the outrageous. Despite his virtual minority-of-one status, he secured public office and managed to hold on, despite the unleashed fury of the local Democrats. He also performed one feat that deserves a statue in Balboa Park.

II

JOSHUA SLOANE'S RISE as a politician dates from 1856. In that year, the Republican Party emerged from the turmoil over slavery and was dedicated to stopping the extension of slavery into the territories. The fledgling party put up John C. Fremont as its presidential candidate to oppose the Democrats' James Buchanan.

In San Diego, Joshua Sloane cheered the new party. He was nearly alone. His backwash town was a den of zealous Southern-sympathizing Democrats. They controlled town politics, and the corrupt Democratic machine ran California like a private club. Undaunted, Sloane called for a Republican rally.

Only two participants are known to have shown up. This anti-slavery, pro-Fremont gathering attracted Sloane and his dog, Patrick. Unfazed by this dismal turn-out, Josh had the presence of mind to record the historic event, the founding of the Republican Party in San Diego.

Sloane penned a letter to Republican National Headquarters. He noted that those present were unanimous in selecting him as county chairman. Needing a secretary, Sloane informed the party leaders that those attending had chosen a certain "Mr. Patrick." However, as Buchanan swamped Fremont, the Sloane-Patrick duo received no emolument that year from party bigwigs.

Joshua Sloane and his dog, Mr. Patrick

In 1859, by some as yet undiscovered skullduggery, Sloane wangled an appointment as Postmaster of San Diego. With the Democratic Postmaster General of the United States supposedly controlling such appointments, this ranks as one of Josh's little political miracles. Local Democrats were furious. They asked, how did this "one-eyed Tomcat" snatch this high-paying position?

His Democratic detractors called a mass meeting to do Josh in. Complaints about postal service were angrily aired. They drew up a petition, addressed to the Postmaster General, listing Sloane's shortcomings. Denouncing him as a "black Republican, incompetent, and a heavy drinker," they demanded his immediate recall. After all the signatures of the party faithful were affixed, the bulky document was deposited at the Post Office.

Later, Postmaster Sloane held the envelope in his hand. He noted its address. Aware of the previous night's meeting, to which he had pointedly not been invited, he suspected this letter was inimical to his own best interest. Always inventive, he discussed with his dog the idea of steaming open the envelope over a tea kettle. As the county secretary of the Republican Party, "Mr. Patrick," voiced no objection to his scheme, Josh proceeded to open the flap.

Sure enough. The letter contained a scathing attack. Most creative in dark moments, Josh took the offensive. He took pen in hand and in elegant, liquored prose launched a panegyric of kudos on the administration of Postmaster Sloane. The document took weighty note of Sloane's popularity, competence, and temperance. He coolly replaced the denigrating statement with his eulogy, pasted the list of signatures below, sealed the envelope, and sent it off on the next steamer.

In time, back came a congratulatory letter from Washington. Delighted that such an estimable postmaster toiled for the department in the hinterlands, the Postmaster General forwarded his best wishes. After informing "Mr. Patrick" of the cheery development, Josh nailed the letter to the outside of his Post Office. With concealed glee, he waited for Democrats to come by and read the dispatch, so he could watch their jaws drop and eyes pop.

In 1860, the political stock of the remarkable Mr. Sloane continued to rise. Abraham Lincoln moved his family into the White House, and party henchmen didn't forget Joshua Sloane and "Mr. Patrick" in far-away San Diego. Josh became Collector of Customs for the harbor and "Mr. Patrick," his Deputy Collector.

Sloane may have suffered second thoughts about

his canine on the Federal payroll. But he didn't notify Washington of the oddity, apparently concluding that, since the new administration had a Civil War on its hands, a lengthy and convoluted explanation could only slow the war effort.

The two bureaucrats divided up the duties of the post. By inclination, Josh sat in his wharf office, waiting for ships' captains to pay their port registration fees. He also kept a pair of opera glasses handy to view pretty females aboard ship. Legend has a less inhibited "Mr. Patrick" making galley inspections, his nose alert for smuggled pork chops.

III

SLOANE'S MOST NOTABLE accomplishment is his least known. In his later years, as a member of the city board of trustees, he championed what is now our cherished Balboa Park. Originally proposed by merchant Ephraim Morse, the idea of setting aside a large tract of land for a future park was taken up by Sloane. With his tart tongue, he badgered his fellow trustees. "Future generations," he taunted, "will know you weren't worth three blind pups if you don't do it."

It worked. In 1870, the board approved reserving 1400 acres for parkland. But the battle wasn't over. Developers hungrily eyed the vast expanse of barren ground for housing. They proposed that portions be cut out for private building. Josh bristled. "I'll be damned if I let them get away with it," he swore. Sloane fought them to a standstill.

In his declining years, Josh was a familiar figure on the boardwalks. He had moved to Alonzo Horton's New Town and lived in a boarding house in what is now downtown San Diego. In the early evening, the dapper little man made his way to his favorite restaurant. There, his table decorated with a good bottle, he lingered fondly over his repast.

The story is told that one evening the elderly Irishman, wending his way slowly back to his bachelor quarters, listed badly to starboard. He paused for friendly support from a roof post over the boardwalk. Just then a holier-than-thou minister happened by. The reverend stared icily at the happily lubricated man and inquired indignantly:

"Mr. Sloane, this is disgraceful. What would you do, if the Lord called for you now?"

Josh pondered the weighty question, his meditation interupted by several untimely hiccups. At length, he solemnly replied, "I don't think I'd go."

.... **OTHER BOOKS AVAILABLE FROM** ......

.... **the same publisher** ....

A Snug Little Purchase, *How Richard Henderson bought Kaintuckee from the Cherokees in 1775*, by Charles Brashers. 1979.
    152pp. illus. paperback $4.95; hardbound $7.95.

Associated Creative Writers also distributes books published by Helix House, Publishers:

1. *Developing Creativity*, by Charles Brashers, 1974. 72pp. illus. paperback only $2.50

2. *Trying to Leave*, poems by Ross Talarico, 1977 48pp. paperback $3.00

3. *Blossoms of the Apricot*, poems by Robert K. Johnson, 1977. 48pp. paperback $3.00

4. *Eight Stories*, by Jerry Bumpus and others, 1975. 140pp. illus. paperback $3.00

ASSOCIATED CREATIVE WRITERS
9231 MOLLY WOODS AVE.,
LA MESA, CA 92041